MW00595872

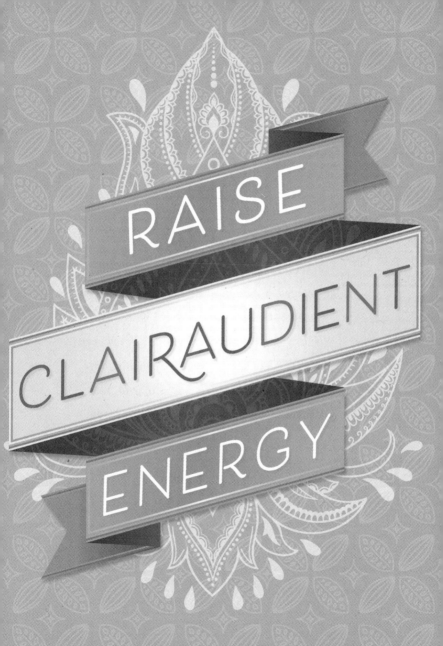

RAISE CLAIRAUDIENT ENERGY

Cyndi Dale

(Minneapolis, MN) is an internationally renowned author, speaker, healer, and business consultant. She is president of Life Systems Services, through which she has conducted over 65,000 client sessions and presented training classes throughout Europe, Asia, and the Americas. Visit her online at CyndiDale.com.

Cyndi Dale's
---ESSENTIAL---
ENERGY
LIBRARY

RAISE

CLAIRAUDIENT

ENERGY

CYNDI DALE

Llewellyn Publications
WOODBURY, MINNESOTA

FIRST EDITION
First Printing, 2018

Book design by Rebecca Zins
Cover design by Ellen Lawson
Illustrations on page 50 and 202 © Mary Ann Zapalac
Llewellyn Publications is a registered trademark
of Llewellyn Worldwide Ltd.

Library of Congress Cataloging-in-Publication Data
Names: Dale, Cyndi, author.
Title: Raise clairaudient energy / Cyndi Dale.
Description: FIRST EDITION. | Woodbury : Llewellyn Worldwide, Ltd., 2018. |
   Series: Cyndi Dale's essential energy library ; # 3 | Includes
   bibliographical references.
Identifiers: LCCN 2018031426 (print) | LCCN 2018036009 (ebook) | ISBN
   9780738755311 (ebook) | ISBN 9780738751634 (alk. paper)
Subjects: LCSH: Clairaudience.
Classification: LCC BF1338 (ebook) | LCC BF1338 .D35 2018 (print) |
   DDC
   133.8/5—dc23
LC record available at https://lccn.loc.gov/2018031426

Llewellyn Worldwide Ltd. does not participate in, endorse, or have any authority or responsibility concerning private business transactions between our authors and the public.

All mail addressed to the author is forwarded, but the publisher cannot, unless specifically instructed by the author, give out an address or phone number.

Any internet references contained in this work are current at publication time, but the publisher cannot guarantee that a specific location will continue to be maintained. Please refer to the publisher's website for links to authors' websites and other sources.

Llewellyn Publications
A Division of Llewellyn Worldwide Ltd.
2143 Wooddale Drive
Woodbury, MN 55125-2989

www.llewellyn.com

Printed in the United States of America

Table of
—CONTENTS—

●   ●   ●   ●   ●   ●

CHAPTER TWO

The Clairaudient's Toolkit: Concepts and Techniques   55

●   ●   ●   ●

• • • • • •

CHAPTER THREE

Classical Clairaudience 99

• • • •

CONTENTS

● ● ● ● ● ●

CHAPTER FOUR

Speaking in Tongues 145

• • • • • •

CHAPTER FIVE

Clairaudient Writing 161

• • • •

CONTENTS

• • • • • •

CHAPTER SIX

Clairaudient Telepathy: Changing Empathy into Telepathy 179

• • • •

●　●　●　●　●　●
CHAPTER SEVEN

Natural Clairaudience: Communing with Nature 211

● ● ● ● ● ●

CHAPTER EIGHT

Healing and Manifesting Through Clairaudience 249

● ● ● ●

CONTENTS

DISCLAIMER

The information in this book is not intended to be used to diagnose or treat any medical or emotional condition. To address medical or therapeutic issues, please consult a licensed professional.

The author and publisher are not responsible for any conditions that require a licensed professional, and we encourage you to consult a professional if you have any questions about the use or efficacy of the techniques or insights in this book. References in this book are given for informational purposes alone and do not constitute an endorsement.

All case studies and descriptions of persons have been changed or altered so as to be unrecognizable. Any likeness to actual persons, living or dead, is strictly coincidental.

INTRODUCTION

I was only five years old when I heard bacon sizzling in the kitchen in the middle of the night. Despite the crackling and hissing, my parents remained asleep. My sisters were in their beds; they too continued to snooze. You see, as I lay in my bedroom down the hall from the kitchen, I was hearing sounds that no one else could hear.

Terrified, but also sort of fascinated, I listened as two hobos discussed the reason they'd jumped off the train that ran behind our house in Huntsville, Alabama, and made their way into our kitchen. I had missed the opening of the door and the shuffling of their shoes, but I could have heard that bacon frying miles away.

Apparently, they frequently stopped at our house. The eggs and milk were fresh, and there was always bacon in the refrigerator. As they laughed about a few of their adventures, I lay frozen, unsure about what to do. Should I spring out of bed and confront them? Wake my parents? Join in the fun?

The decision was made when I heard the clinking of the dishes and frying pan against the steel sink. Then the kitchen door slammed. The house was quiet; they had left. I had only two thoughts.

The first was that my mom would be furious about the dirty dishes in the sink. The second was that my parents should get a better lock system. I ran into my parents' room and yelled at them to wake up.

My mom was angry—but with me, not the hobos. She hated being disturbed in the middle of the night. My dad traipsed into the kitchen and pronounced it pristine. He then grumbled, telling me to stop "making things up." It was at that point when I figured out that my kitchen visitors had been ghosts.

I've heard sounds that others can't—or won't—all my life. These days, as an energy healer and intuitive consultant, I assist my clients by listening to an array of invisible informants, including my clients' spiritual guides, angelic guardians, and deceased loved ones. Also in the lineup are problematic entities and aspects of my clients' personalities, such as inner children or past-life selves. On a client's behalf, I've consulted invisible oracles from the future and shamans long dead. I've heard tell of needed healing energies and possible future events. Almost any type of information is available through clairaudience, a word that means "clear hearing." Using my clairaudience, along with other spiritual abilities, I've helped over 65,000 clients.

As implied, the professional application of my clairaudient gift is an extension of my childhood proclivities. I also come by it naturally, through both sides of my family.

On my dad's side, my grandmother used to communicate with ghosts. One of her favorite "friends" was a spirit who hung out in her house, sharing cooking recipes. My grandmother would also relay conversations she held with my grandfather after he died. One time, my grandfather spoke to my grandmother through the television, which wasn't turned on, sharing his sorrow for the hurt he'd caused her when alive.

My mother's side was a bit more colorful in their apparitional dealings. Apparently one Norwegian ancestress was so vocal about her psychic undertakings that she was hung for witchcraft. Another forefather, a writer, was known to constantly mumble at unseen companions. Who knows who he was talking to—or exactly which invisible characters were really writing his books?

Did you hear what others couldn't hear when you were a child? Did you start perceiving psychic shout-outs as an adult? Perhaps your clairaudient ability has been a consistent part of your life or an intergenerational pattern. Then again, you might be clairaudient but not know it. These variations—and the possible confusion—exist because clairaudient sounds are considerably varied. They can resonate inside the mind or enter through the ears. They can consist of words, statements, dialogue, or even humming, chanting, musical notations, loud sounds, whispers, poetic recitations, or other forms of vocalizations and verbalizations.

Complicating—and enriching—the clairaudient phenomenon is the fact that psychic sounds can be packaged as mundane or supernatural. A much-needed message might be delivered via an audible blip in a television commercial or a bird chirping outside your window. Then again, it could be dispensed through a ghost, angel, or even an aspect of yourself that speaks entirely within your mind. And while most clairaudient messages are communicated verbally, others are delivered through writing. Other sound bites must be decoded from a bodily sensation or feeling. No matter your experience with clairaudience, the most reassuring aspect of the gift is that by further developing it, you can access the visible and invisible beings that stand ready to inform, instruct, and inspire.

To clarify, clairaudience is one of several major mystical gifts. The other main groupings are clairvoyance, or "clear seeing," and clairempathy, or "clear knowing." This book is the third in a series showcasing ways to employ subtle energy—also called psychic, spiritual, or mystical energy—to create more joy, love, and prosperity for yourself and others. Together, the first three books in my Essential Energy Library reveal easy and safe ways to interact mystically for everyday benefits.

Your Three Major Mystical Gifts
THE "SISTERS CLAIR"

This book is about clairaudience, the art of clearly hearing messages intuitively. What's exciting is that clairaudience is one of three major mystical or intuitive gifts, all of which are available to help you gain spiritual guidance, perform healing, and attract opportunities. In fact, I like to picture clairaudience as a member of a three-part family that I call the "clairs." The other two "sisters" are clairvoyance and clairempathy.

All members of this special sisterhood operate energetically. Energy is information that moves, and there are two types: subtle and physical. These three mystical sisters specialize in subtle energy, which is also called psychic, mystical, intuitive, and spiritual energy. This is the energy that comprises the unexplainable, supernatural, and extraordinary. This is the stuff that is ruled by the three clairs, each of which constructs physical reality with subtle energies.

As stated, clairaudience involves sending and receiving psychic information that can be heard inside our head or through our ears. Clairvoyance describes our innate ability to perceive psychic visions. And clairempathy empowers us to sense, feel, know, and be aware of what's occurring in the subtle realms. There are actually several types of clairempathy, as this is the most complicated of the gifts.

All three of the clairs function through the subtle energy anatomy, which is composed of the subtle organs, fields, and channels that form our essential self. The subtle organs called the chakras are the most important to understand for those seeking to use their mystical gifts. Besides being able to transform subtle energy into physical energy and vice versa, each chakra serves as a sort of "throne room" for a clair. In other words, each chakra relates to a specific mystical function, helping you intuitively communicate with the world.

Want to become better acquainted with the clairs and their related intuitive faculties? Let me introduce you. I'll describe each clair and also the chakra/s and intuitive abilities that it manages. You'll learn a lot more about chakras in this book.

SISTER ONE: **Clairaudience.** Clear hearing. Employs the fifth chakra, the communication center in the throat.

SISTER TWO: **Clairvoyance.** Clear seeing. Taps into the sixth chakra, the visual center in the brow.

SISTER THREE: **Clairempathy.** Clear relating. There are several types of clairempathy, each of which is based in a different chakra. Following is a brief description of the various forms of clairempathy in terms of how they help us relate to the outside world:

- *Physical empathy:* Sensing others' physical energy in our own body. First chakra.

- *Emotional empathy:* Feeling others' emotions inside ourselves. Second chakra.

- *Mental empathy:* Knowing what others know. Third chakra.

- *Relational empathy:* Awareness of others'
  relational and healing needs. Fourth chakra.
- *Spiritual empathy:* Sensitivity to others' spiritual
  desires and needs. Seventh chakra.

Isn't it fun to know you have access to all three types of mystical gifts? You'll be learning more about all of these gifts as they relate to clairaudience in this book.

• • •

The reason that we can access the extraordinary is that we are innately equipped with the mechanics for operating energetically. Why wouldn't we be? Everything in this world, seen and unseen, is composed of energy, which is vibrating information. Even more pointedly, energy functions on two levels: physical and subtle, as do we. We employ our two basic energetic anatomies, physical and subtle, to communicate through our normal but also psychic senses. These two structures work together to enable visual, empathic, and verbal psychic activity.

In this book you'll be specifically educated about the physical and subtle energy systems that underlie clairaudience, or verbal psychism. This knowledge will help you manage these systems, especially your subtle structure, so you can further awaken and employ every type of clairaudience.

In all, there are six types of clairaudience, and I'll instruct you in each. Don't be surprised if you're better at performing certain styles rather than others. After all, we each differ in personality, background, and capacity. With this caveat in mind, I recommend that you learn about and practice all the clairaudient capabilities outlined in this book. Who knows what you'll latch onto now rather than later? Why not develop all facets of your clairaudient gift, no matter where you're starting from? What you don't use now might come in handy later.

Your journey begins in chapter 1, which lays the groundwork for understanding clairaudience. I'll first provide a basic definition of the gift and then lead you on a whirlwind tour through history, showcasing a few of the famous greats who used their clairaudient abilities to contribute to the world. I'll then briefly describe the six basic styles of clairaudience, each of which will be featured in a later chapter, and finally excavate the physical and subtle science of clairaudience.

In chapter 2 you'll acquire the concepts and techniques necessary to develop each of the six clairaudient styles. Featured is a discussion about what clairaudience is and what it isn't. Namely, clairaudience is not a mental illness, nor does it involve stress-induced hallucinations, although people with these challenges can sometimes hear what others can't hear. Distinguishing between authentic clairaudient experiences and other phenomena is an important part of gaining confidence in your psychic abilities. By the time you leave chapter 2, you'll have acquired all the principles and processes needed to assure safe travels on every clairaudient excursion.

Thus equipped, we'll move into the core of the book. Each of the next six chapters is devoted to helping you cultivate one of the main clairaudient styles. Every chapter will thoroughly examine a specific style, share examples and applicable scientific information, and present techniques for activating and applying the style.

The chapters and their related clairaudient styles are described next.

CLASSICAL CLAIRAUDIENCE (CHAPTER 3): The art of mediumship or channeling, divided into three categories, which are full, partial, and receptive. This chapter includes discussions about connecting with the living and the dead, as well as with spiritual beings. It even shows you how to conduct a séance. Know that most of the pointers and tips presented in this chapter are pertinent to the following chapters, as many clairaudient activities employ channeling.

● ● ●

SPEAKING IN TONGUES (CHAPTER 4): The ability to bring through or understand other languages, whether they are earthly or heavenly. You'll learn two basic forms of tongue speaking.

● ● ●

CLAIRAUDIENT WRITING (CHAPTER 5): The use of writing to gain mystical wisdom. This chapter will present two forms of psychic writing. You'll also be shown how to send healing and good tidings through written communication.

● ● ●

TELEPATHIC EMPATHY (CHAPTER 6): Empathy is the awareness of psychic messages in the body. Telepathic empathy involves transforming these sensations into auditory messages. We'll look at four types of telepathy, which are primal, feeling-based, mental, and spiritual.

● ● ●

NATURAL CLAIRAUDIENCE (CHAPTER 7): The
means of communicating with beings from the
natural world. There are two basic categories
of natural beings, which are earthly and otherworldly. In this chapter you'll explore everything
from picking up on your pet's needs to connecting with an extraterrestrial.

* * *

HEALING AND MANIFESTING (CHAPTER 8): We
all want better lives, which is accomplished by
reducing negativity and opening to positivity.
This chapter features several ways to accomplish
both activities through applications of clairaudience.

* * *

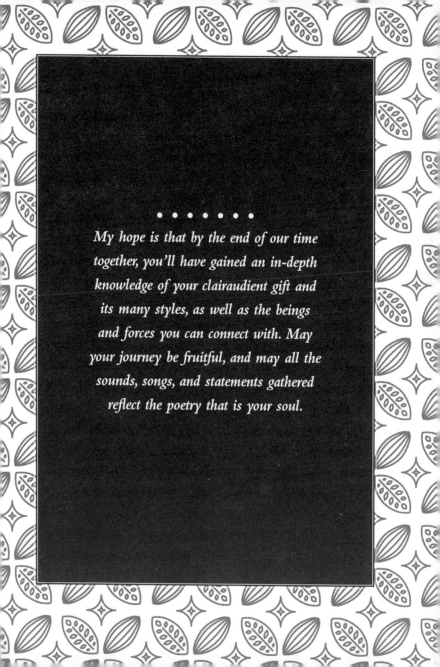

• • • • • • •

*My hope is that by the end of our time
together, you'll have gained an in-depth
knowledge of your clairaudient gift and
its many styles, as well as the beings
and forces you can connect with. May
your journey be fruitful, and may all the
sounds, songs, and statements gathered
reflect the poetry that is your soul.*

As you move through this book, you'll discover that some of our discussions might feel a little more "out there" than those you have on a daily basis. Think about it. How often do you sit around and talk about extraterrestrials or fairies? Several years ago these types of conversations might have startled me. Can aliens really communicate with us? Are there really invisible beings in nature with whom we can interface? Is it actually possible to connect with beings from other dimensions or talk with an angel?

Through my own experiences, as well as those of the thousands of people with whom I've worked, I've come to believe that these types of considerations are genuine and authentic. In fact, covering these types of "airy-fairy" issues (pun intended) is critical for gaining an understanding of clairaudience. Through your clairaudient gift, you can potentially dial up thousands of concrete and other-worldly beings that aren't listed in a telephone directory. Of course, you'll want to interface with certain beings rather than others. Nonetheless, I encourage you to remain open-minded, knowing that you get to personally select the data and beings you want to connect with or not.

Given the sometimes ethereal nature of clairaudience, I've worked to make sure that this book is as usable and beneficial as possible. To meet that goal, I've included plenty of exercises. These will assist you in doing everything from communicating with the deceased to speaking in another language. These processes will frequently employ the two techniques that I feature the most often in my books, including the books in this series. These techniques are called Spirit-to-Spirit and Healing Streams of Grace.

If you are new to these techniques, you'll be happy to learn about them. They can be applied toward meeting any life goal, including healing, manifesting, and decision-making. They can also help you secure energetic protection, attract love, and obtain spiritual guidance. If you are already acquainted with these methods, great! You'll be acquiring yet another use for these procedures: that of developing your clairaudience.

CHAPTER ONE

What Is Clairaudience?

Every journey starts with getting a lay of the land, and that's the purpose of this chapter. Here I'll map out the understandings needed to safely develop your clairaudient talent.

First off, I'll present different ways to look at clairaudience and then close in on a working definition. Since all subjects are easier to comprehend within a historical context, I'll next flip through the pages of time to introduce a few famous clairaudient greats and their feats. This study will uncover the deep roots of clairaudience, revealing the role that it has played in religion, philosophy, and the arts, among other topic areas. Reading about how others have used their clairaudient talents might suggest ways that you can employ your own clairaudient capabilities.

Next, I'll outline the six basic categories of clairaudient expression. This endeavor is really important because many people think that clairaudience is limited to hearing the deceased. Certainly clairaudience can be applied toward this task, but there are many other clairaudient undertakings—wait until you see them all! And then, finally, we'll peruse the physical and subtle sciences, seeking to explain clairaudient phenomena.

As you'll discover in this chapter, clairaudience is possible because we are energetic beings. The words, songs, tones, and full-on proclamations we psychically hear through our clairaudient gift exist because we can process physical and subtle messages. Attune your energetic capabilities and you can better tune in to your clairaudient genius.

The Sounds of Silence
TOWARD A WORKING DEFINITION OF CLAIRAUDIENCE

When I was a freshman in college, a professor posed a famous philosophical question to the class: If a tree falls in the forest and no one is around to hear it, does it make a sound?

It took a while, but I realized that the authenticity of a noise isn't dependent on who or what might hear it. A sound is a sound is a sound. That statement also applies to the clairaudient, who might be the only person actually aware of a sound, or at least of the meaning held within it.

The term *clairaudience*, which means "clear hearing," was first coined in the late seventeenth century in France to describe the ability to receive messages from the dead. This is the facet of clairaudience that pops into most people's minds when seeking to define clairaudience, along with imagery like darkened rooms, foggy air, an entranced medium, and eerie messages. The faculty is much broader than merely conversing with members of the afterlife, however. Clairaudients are potentially able to hear all sorts of meaningful sounds, whether these sounds are heard only inside of the head or enter through the ears as psychic or environmental noises. When someone is truly open to clairaudient dispatches, they can receive all three types of communiqués, sometimes from the same source.

For instance, I once received a clairaudient message from my deceased father in a dream. Within my mind, he told me that I needed a new furnace. My father had been a trustworthy handyman, so in the morning I called the utility company. They sent a technician out right away. After checking my furnace, he pronounced that it would die within days.

I was ordering the delivery and installation of a new furnace for a week out when I heard a loud bang. So did the technician, who said, "Maybe we should do this sooner." He laughed, but it was obvious that my father had used an environmental noise to make a point. After scheduling the appointment for the next day, I heard a cry of glee as if from someone standing right next to me. The technician's face remained blank; he hadn't heard a peep. Given the rather ghostly nature of my father's presence, I was glad that I was the only person who perceived my father's confirmation of the delivery date.

As these examples reveal, clairaudience is a multilayered mystical gift that can present itself in many ways. Clairaudient sources are equally complex, including physical beings, such as people and animals, but also nonphysical beings, such as angels, saints, spiritual guides, masters, the deceased, demons, extraterrestrials, fairies, and the like. As stated, clairaudient messages can be generated by another living person but also by a part of one, such as their soul or mind, or even aspects of yourself, such as the "you" from a past life.

To complicate matters further, clairaudient messages, while frequently packaged as words or sentences, can also be presented as noises, chants, tones, ringing bells, slamming doors, whispers, screams, or any other sound. And these and other clairaudient sounds, whether perceived psychically or environmentally, can do so much more than deliver a message. They can also be used to perform healing and manifesting.

Of course, not every sound, whether it is perceived in the mind or through the ears, contains or evokes a deeper meaning. Sometimes a sound is a sound, nothing more. A banging door might actually slam because you didn't shut it all the way. The voice in your head might be a worry, not a spiritual message. You could drive yourself crazy seeking significance in every little noise or thought. It is for this reason that I like to define clairaudience in the following way, which is broad enough to encompass its many facets and narrow enough to be practical:

> *Clairaudience involves receiving or sending meaningful verbal messages that are psychic in nature or beyond the range of human hearing. Nonetheless, these sounds can be packaged in audible sounds.*

The keyword is "psychic," which is a form of energy that, as you'll learn about in this chapter, moves either faster or slower than its cousin, the more easily perceived physical energy. Other terms for "psychic" include subtle, spiritual, and mystical, but the bottom line is that a sound is just a sound, whether it is audible to others or not, unless it contains a meaningful message—and then, when the sound is potent and important, it's a doorway into the universe.

Walk down memory lane with me, and I'll show you what I mean.

Clairaudience Through the Ages
A HISTORY OF THE GIFT

As you'll discover in this section, across time clairaudience has been one of the most natural and vital skills experienced by humans. Not only that, it has served as a delivery vehicle for many of the world's greatest achievements, serving as the backbone of nearly every religious and spiritual discipline, but also of secular triumphs in philosophy, literature, and music.

It's actually hard to pinpoint a religion that isn't familiar with or dependent on clairaudience. For instance, the founders of all three Abrahamic religions—Judaism, Christianity, and Islam—based many of their perceptions on clairaudient revelations, which they believed originated from God or a godly messenger.

Consider how often God speaks with Adam in the Judeo-Christian text. In Genesis, for example, we find

God counseling Adam about how to act in the Garden of Eden (Genesis 2: 16-17). Later, Adam and Eve hear God walking and talking in the garden, right before God admonishes them for giving into temptation (Genesis 3: 8-19). And the clairaudient advice goes on and on. As time ensues, God tells Moses how to free the Hebrews from slavery and also informs Noah that the tides are rising. Time to build a boat! A cursory reading finds dozens of other male and female prophets, judges, and followers clued into God's opinions and wisdom through clairaudiently delivered words, dreams, prayers, angelic decrees, chiseled tablets, and even a burning bush.

The Christian New Testament is also replete with examples of clairaudience. Jesus constantly converses with God, but he is not the only recipient of the Holy One's words. After being crucified, Jesus speaks to Saul, a Jew who is killing Christians. Clairaudiently communicating with Saul, Jesus asks, "Why do you persecute me?" (Acts 9:4). Saul's heart softens and he later travels far and wide to spread the news of God's love.

Would Islam even exist if not for clairaudience? The answer is no, as the religion began when Muhammad received a visit from Archangel Gabriel. During their meeting, Gabriel asked Muhammad to "read" five special verses. The word "read" doesn't describe an actual reading of written words; rather, Gabriel recited the verses even as Allah inscribed them on Muhammad's heart. This way, Muhammad would always remember and understand them.

Collectively, the five verses clarified Islam as a religion of peace and beauty, but I believe that one of the verses in particular reveals the ultimate function of clairaudience. As stated, "He who taught the use of the pen, taught man that which he knew not" (Al-Islam.org, n.d.). At the purest level, isn't clairaudience exactly what these words convey—a means to unveil universal truths?

Most religious devotees would agree, although not every recipient of a clairaudient revelation has personally benefited from a spiritual download. Perhaps the most famous case in point is Joan of Arc, a clairaudient and clairvoyant prodigy born in 1412.

At twelve years old, Joan began hearing the voices of spiritual guides, including Archangel Michael. Ultimately, these messages were presented to the Dauphin of France, who then asked Joan to lead the French army against the English. Though the French won because of Joan's heroism, she was burned at the stake as a heretic when she was only eighteen. Joan's demise points out one of the reasons that some people are scared of their clairaudient gifts. Historically, the mystical gifts have sometimes been more feared than revered and punished instead of rewarded.

The Abrahamic religions aren't the only spiritual discipline nourished by clairaudience. The world's oldest religion, Hinduism, is almost entirely based on insights revealed to the rishis, wise men with clairaudient and other mystical gifts. Even now, the Hindus believe that seekers attain supernatural powers upon enlightenment, including advanced clairaudience.

One religion of particular interest in relation to clairaudience is Spiritualism. Spiritualism is marked by the belief that the living can communicate with the dead. The most famous Spiritualist was Emanuel Swedenborg, a seventeenth-century mystic and scientist. By his own accounting, Swedenborg frequently spoke with angels and spirits in the same way that he conversed with people. He was most likely one of the most formidable mediums, bar none (Mowbray 2018).

Personally, I've always been captivated by the spiritual beliefs of indigenous healers and mystics. In my own travels, I've connected with shamans from Peru, Costa Rica, Belize, Morocco, Japan, Venezuela, and dozens of other cultures, each of whom attribute their healing powers to their ability to psychically hear and see the spirits of the deceased, the land, and the heavens. Though these cultures hold distinct spiritual beliefs and practices, they have all expressed that the ultimate goal of clairaudience, as well as the other clairs, is to connect people to "the One."

Clairaudience has contributed to secular society as well. Consider the famous philosopher Socrates, who could hear a voice that wasn't his own since childhood. Calling it his "daemonic sign," Socrates insisted that its advice prevented him from making mistakes, such as entering politics. (We could only hope that others might start hearing that same voice.) Others became jealous of this daemon voice, however, and brought Socrates to court, where it was decreed that his clairaudient voice was "unlicensed" because it was the equivalent of a new god (McCarthy-Jones 2012, 19).

There are endless numbers of other people whose clairaudient abilities have benefited themselves and others. Probably few individuals know that when living alone in a new city, psychiatrist Sigmund Freud would hear a beloved voice calling his name, providing him comfort. Peacemaker Gandhi heeded a voice from afar that released him from inner struggles, and for years poet William Blake conferred with a deceased friend, who helped him with his personal life and writings (Hearing Voices Network 2018). Then there is Charles Dickens, the famous novelist, who wasn't shy about attributing stories to his invisible companions, with whom he often chatted.

As to be expected, many of the world's most beautiful musical scores were actually composed in the heavens, or at the least delivered by heavenly inhabitants. Composer Robert Schumann is one of my favorite examples. Living between 1810 and 1856, Schumann was delighted to be visited one night by the ghost of Schubert. While listening, he wrote down Schubert's composition. After this experience, Schumann reported hearing the voices of angelic choirs. Unfortunately, he also started hearing demonic voices (Hearing Voices Network, n.d.).

We can't deliberate clairaudience without mentioning American mystic Edgar Cayce. Living between 1877 and 1945, Cayce channeled answers to questions while he was in a trance state. Much of the time, his advice was directed at improving a client's health. Succinctly, Cayce believed he gathered information from an unlimited pool of data called the Akashic Records, which registered sound and vibration from across time (Near-Death Experiences and the Afterlife 2016). Whatever name is used to label the universal library of wisdom and knowledge, it is available to everyone through their clairaudience.

We can't complete our historical outing without scrutinizing the darker side of clairaudience. For an example, we don't have to look any further than Adolf Hitler.

It is well known that Hitler could hear a voice, which he attributed to Divine Providence. The "Voice," as he labeled it, saved his life many times. For example, it instructed him to leave a trench in which he was eating with fellow soldiers during World War I. He did. Moments later, that part of the trench was shelled. Everyone who'd been previously sitting around him was killed.

This same voice had spoken to him when he was only seventeen. It told him he would become the savior of Germany. Moreover, his friend, who was with him at the time, heard the voice from Hitler's mouth and determined that young Hitler was possessed by an external entity. Over time, his military compatriots also came to believe that he was a crazed medium who was controlled by external forces (Joseph 1996).

Yes, there are good and bad sounds and voices, and we'll discuss how to differentiate between them in the next chapter. In order to make use of that information, it's important to understand the various types of clairaudient gifts. Discerning between positive and negative sources and information can depend on the style that you are employing. The following section outlines the six main types of clairaudient faculties. As you read through them, see if you can perceive yourself in any or many of these categories.

Types of Clairaudience

Following are the six broad categories of clairaudience. Each of these styles will parallel one of the chapters between 3 and 8. In those chapters I'll more fully explore the featured variety of clairaudience. Besides expanding the descriptions and teaching techniques, I'll also share particular scientific and psychological views about that clairaudient type, if applicable.

The six categories include:

1: Classical Clairaudience

Classical clairaudience is the type we most commonly affiliate with the verbal psychic gift. Basically, classical clairaudience involves hearing words, chants, tones, noises, or any other sound from a human, whether dead or alive, or an otherworldly source, including angels and masters. The sounds also can be generated from aspects of a person or an entity, or even a group of people or entities. An entity is a being that has a unique soul and personality. Technically that definition encompasses living people as well as nonhuman beings.

These sounds can be perceived as internally or externally generated and generally come when someone is in a trance state, although there are many types of trance states. We'll explore this concept in chapter 3.

Classical clairaudience is based on mediumship or channeling, which are two interchangeable terms. Also used is the word *transmediumship*. Mediums or channels literally serve as a conduit between realms, with the channeler acting as a pass-through for an entity or group of entities. Channeling is also the foundation of many types of clairaudience, as most clairaudient activities involve making psychic connections. However, there are differing levels of mediumship or channeling, which I'll describe next.

FULL MEDIUMSHIP/CHANNELING: During a full mediumship activity, the soul of the person exits their own body while another entity or group of entities enters and communicates verbally. While this happens, the soul of the person is in the part of the self that travels from one existence to another, or one lifetime to another, to gain experience and learn about love. Sometimes I call this type of channeling "clear channeling," as the channel's personality is cleared out to make way for the incoming entity.

This is the mediumship most commonly affiliated with séances.

As you will learn in the next chapter, there are downsides to full mediumship. Having another soul inside is quite physically stressful. We can't process energies that aren't our own. At several points in the book, I'll describe ways to recognize the red flags of full channeling and avoid its serious dangers.

PARTIAL MEDIUMSHIP/CHANNELING: Partial channeling occurs when a medium allows an entity or group of entities to co-inhabit their body. In other words, during partial channeling your soul shares space with at least one other soul. If you're performing this type of channeling, you'll be fully present in your body but also be able to hear and feel the other entity or energies within you. As a case in point, I was once working on a client when a saint entered my body. His energy flowed from my hands into the client. My client immediately felt better and later stated that she was happier for months afterward. Because the saint had also shared its healing energy with me, I felt more buoyant for weeks after the saint exited.

RECEPTIVE MEDIUMSHIP/CHANNELING: This is by far the easiest type of channeling to perform, and it is also the safest. When performing receptive channeling, your soul remains fully vested in your body and you receive clairaudient messages from an entity or several entities that remain outside of your body. I use this type of channeling more than any other. For instance, within a single client session, I might hear a communiqué from a client's deceased mother, talk to the client's soul about a past life, or listen to the client's spiritual guide.

We'll explore all versions of mediumship, also learning about trance states and séances, in chapter 3.

2: Speaking in Tongues

The most famous example of this type of clairaudience occurred on Pentecost about 2,000 years ago, when tongues of holy fire fell upon Jesus and his followers. The people then "spoke in tongues," or talked in different languages. Technically, tongue speaking is a specialized version of channeling.

You'll be introduced to two types of tongue speaking in this book:

DIVINE SPEAKING: Called *glossolalia*, divine speaking involves speaking in tongues in a language so divine that humans can't usually understand it. The language coming through the speaker might be stated, sung, chanted, hummed, or otherwise delivered verbally.

LANGUAGE SPEAKING: Formally called *xenoglossy*, this activity involves bringing through a foreign language or an accent that wasn't previously known. Most of the time these languages are earthly, although they can also be otherworldly. Yes, beings from other planets might want to talk through you for a while! During language speaking, the clairaudient and listener/s might or might not understand the message being shared.

In chapter 4 I'll provide in-depth instruction in tongue speaking.

3: Clairaudient Writing

What if you could sit down and compose a piece of prose, poetry, or song with the help of an invisible expert? You can. Clairaudient writing is probably one of the easiest of the clairaudient gifts to develop, and there are two main styles, guided and automatic.

> GUIDED WRITING: Guided writing is similar to receptive channeling in that your soul remains in your body while wisdom, poetry, music, or some other creative effort pours through you. The main difference is that you are writing the message. Less frequently, the process can be accomplished through partial channeling, which involves sharing your body with an external entity or entities.

> AUTOMATIC WRITING: In this activity, your soul partially or fully exits your body and a different being enters. It then uses your physicality to write a message.

In chapter 5 I'll present the safest ways to conduct both forms of clairaudient writing. I'll also show you how to generate and send healing energy through clairaudient writing.

4: Telepathic Empathy

Telepathy is usually defined as the ability to hear another's thoughts. I actually work with four types of telepathy, and yes, "mental empathy," or mind-to-mind communication, is one of them.

Telepathic abilities frequently start with a form of empathy, or clairempathy, and involve transforming an empathic knowing into verbal insights. In chapter 6 you'll learn about the four basic types of telepathy:

PRIMAL TELEPATHY: Primal empathy, also called physical empathy, is our most fundamental instinct, relying on bodily sensations to alert us to danger or opportunity. It's far easier to understand the meaning of a physical reaction after converting it to a verbal message, thereby forming the basis of primal telepathy.

FEELING TELEPATHY: There are five feeling constellations or groupings: sadness, fear, anger, disgust, and joy. When we're emotionally empathic, we're tuning in to our body's feelings and trying to figure out what they mean, as each feeling constellation delivers a different message. The emotional message might be our own, but we also

might have absorbed someone else's emotions.
No matter the case, it's far easier to comprehend an emotional sensation if we turn it into a
clairaudient message. This conversion is the basis
of feeling telepathy.

MENTAL TELEPATHY: Through mental empathy,
we relate to our own and others' thoughts and
beliefs. There are two styles of mental telepathy.
The first is true mind-to-mind communication and involves the transference of another's
thoughts to our own brain. This occurs through
our fifth chakra, a subtle energy center that
processes communication. (We'll be exploring
chakras later in this chapter.) The second activity
is empathic and involves receiving another's
mental impressions, which we must then translate into a verbal message. This process utilizes
our third chakra, the center of mental empathy.

I once experienced mental telepathy years
ago when working out at the health club. The
name of the man using the machine next to me
jumped into my head. We chatted, and I discovered that I was correct. Years later, after my
divorce, I met this man again on match.com.

We didn't officially date, but we did become friends. When we'd get together for coffee, I could easily sense what he believed about various subjects and translate these impressions as words in my head.

The first example I provided about this relationship qualifies as fifth-to-fifth chakra telepathy. The follow-on example, in which I could put words to this man's ideas, used third-to-third chakra telepathy. You'll learn more about both versions of mental telepathy in this book.

SPIRITUAL TELEPATHY: Spiritual empathy occurs when we sense or become aware of a truth known to the Spirit or to a spiritual guide, such as an angel, saint, or guru. Spiritual telepathy raises the bar by transforming a spiritual knowing into a verbal understanding. In the telepathic state, we can literally speak with and for the Spirit.

5: Natural Clairaudience

Have you ever communicated with an animal or a natural being? Maybe you have a strong relationship with an animal, plant, or bird. Or perhaps you'd benefit from translating a message from a fairy or an off-world alien. Through natural clairaudience you can receive messages from and communicate with earthly and otherworldly beings.

We'll explore natural clairaudience in chapter 7.

6: Healing and Manifesting

There are two vital ways to use your clairaudient abilities: healing, which involves releasing unneeded energies, and manifesting, the attraction of desirable energies. A few of the concepts here appeared in the first book in the Essential Energy Library series, *Subtle Energy Techniques*.

You'll learn about healing and manifesting through clairaudience in chapter 8.

You'll notice that I've frequently referenced the fact that psychic messages can be delivered through environmental sounds. Throughout many of these chapters, namely chapters 3, 6, and 7, I'll specifically address how to interpret environmental sounds.

No matter what, all six forms of clairaudience will be easier to accomplish if you understand how clairaudience works, which is the subject of the next section.

The Science of Clairaudience

IT'S A MATTER OF ENERGY

How do we best explain clairaudience? Energetically.

Energy is information that moves or vibrates. Since everything is made of energy, all components of clairaudience, the art of hearing a psychically encoded message, can be explained by this definition. There are, however, two main types of energy: physical and subtle energies. Understanding the differences and similarities between these and the systems that regulate each one is the key to knowing how clairaudience works. And when we comprehend how an activity works, it's far easier to perform it.

Physical energy, best explained by classical science, is relatively measurable, stable, and predictable. If you set a glass on the table before going to bed, it will be there in the morning—unless you live at my house. Then Lucky the yellow lab will knock it over with his tail. Even so, that's a pretty predictable outcome.

Understood through the five senses of sight, hearing, touch, taste, and smell, a physical event is perceived in much the same way by different people. If within hearing range, everyone will hear a knock on the door. Given normal eyesight, all people watching a Western will agree that the cowboys are wearing hats.

Now let's consider subtle energy. As already shared, subtle energy is also called psychic, spiritual, and mystical energy. Unlike physical energy, which is regulated by natural law, subtle energy is best explained by quantum physics, which breaks just about every rule.

Quantum (or subtle) energy can travel at speeds much faster or slower than physical energy. Because of this, subtle messages, including psychic missives, can do almost anything they want—or what we want them to. On the quantum level, time and distance are merely constructs. This means that you can sit in your recliner with your dog at your feet and tune in to a communication from a caveman in the past, send a memo to your future self, and listen to an angel singing in the heavens.

As different as physical and subtle energies seem, they are interconnected. Physical energy can transform into subtle energy and vice versa. In regards to clairaudience, this means that a psychically received sound can be changed into a physically heard sound. For instance, you can pick up the subtle energy of another's thoughts and transform them into words heard in your head. The opposite can also happen. That dog sleeping near your recliner? Let's say it barks. Although you don't speak "dog," you can pull the psychic message out of the physical sound and translate it into your own language.

These conversions are possible because of the interface between our physical and subtle systems, which we'll discuss next.

Structures of Energy
PHYSICAL AND SUBTLE

If you want to fully awaken your clairaudience, it's vital to comprehend the mechanics of sound from physical and subtle perspectives. After examining the technicalities of physical sound, I'll do the same within the subtle arena. Then I'll put my understanding of the two systems together so you're completely ready to dive into your gift development.

The Physical Mechanics of Sound

From a physical point of view (and subtle too, actually), sounds are made by energetic vibrations. When an object vibrates, it creates movement in the surroundings, which pass the vibrations on as sound waves. These waves continue traveling until they run out of energy or strike something. When the latter occurs, a sound is produced. Otherwise the sound waves continue moving without creating an audible noise, although I would personally suggest that the psychic energy carried in or generated by the moving sound waves comprise immeasurable sounds. In order to hear a sound, our physical system has to convert the energy in a sound wave into nerve impulses, or electromagnetic activity. It is these electrical units that our brain then decodes so it can figure out what we're hearing.

There are many ways that sound waves get to the brain. The most classical explanation is that a physical noise enters through the ear canal and then vibrates the ear drum. The resulting vibrations pass through three middle ear bones and stir a fluid that stimulates thousands of hair-like cells, which convert the vibrations into nerve impulses. These impulses are then carried to the brain by the auditory nerve. *Voilà*, the brain deciphers the impulses based on memory, perceived meaning, frequency (pitch), and intensity (loudness). Many people, however, don't realize that there are several other body parts involved in hearing.

In fact, current European researchers are proving that our skull bones are also implicated in hearing, in that they transfer sound vibrations to the temporal bone, which sends the vibrations into the ear canal (Smith 2015). According to the famous audiologist Alfred Tomatis, who died in 2001, all of the body's bones, as well as our skin, are involved in hearing. According to Tomatis, when we talk our skull vibrates and sends sound waves through the spine into the rest of the body, mainly through the bones. These waves also pass into the environment through our skin; hence, we share messages to the world through the sound waves emanating from our body.

When we're listening to sounds, including our own verbalizations, our skin "decides" what sound waves to block or absorb. The skin is actually replete with cells similar to those in the inner ear. Some people are sensitive to certain sounds and not others, meaning they will reject some noises—or require them to be really loud—before the skin invites in the sound waves. After passing the "skin test," incoming sound waves enter our bones, which conduct the waves upward through the spine.

The criteria for our sensitivity starts in the womb, says Tomatis, and depends on our reactions to our mother's sounds. In fact, by seven months in utero, a fetus can respond to the fifty-two phonemes, or units of sound, that create language. Literally, the child will move different muscles or muscle groups in reaction to different phonemes (Dejean, n.d.). Hence, right from the beginning of life, we pay more attention to certain sounds than others. I believe this statement can apply to psychically perceived sounds as well as physical, and it accounts for the reason we're more equipped to perform certain types of clairaudience rather than others—or hear certain types of beings rather than others.

Internal sounds, those we generate and hear inside of our minds, are created through the same systems used to process external speech (Ellis 2013). What's interesting is that scientists are now able to decode a person's internally generated voice. They are accomplishing this task by deciphering the brain's electromagnetic activity using electrodes and computer technology (Swain 2012), whereby the scientists transfer the recordings of a person's brain activity to a computer. These activities are picked up by electrodes connecting the person's head to the computer. Researchers then interpret the meaning of the electrical patterns. I am pointing out this research because I believe it is similar to what occurs when we pick up on others' thoughts. The only difference is that when operating through clairaudience, we are relying on the transference of subtle sound waves rather than physically measurable sound waves. Essentially, our psychic "antennae" can register whatever sounds we're attuned to and decipher them—if we know how.

Having shared this observation, it's time to better understand the subtle system involved in sounding. I can then more formally explain how physical and subtle sounds and energy systems interrelate.

The Subtle Mechanics of Sound

As you learned in the last section, hearing and listening are basically the creation, transference, and interpretation of sound waves and electromagnetic activity, or light. The clairaudient or psychic aspects of hearing occur because the sounds and lights that travel at speeds different than the more discernible physical can be translated as auditory perceptions.

There are several vehicles that transcribe subtle messages as physical sounds and vice versa. One instrument is a set of subtle energies called phonons. Phonons are quantum "sound units" that are organized like crystal lattices. These exist in your body and are especially present in the blood and the organs' cavities. Every time your heart beats or some other pressure wave is set off internally, the phonons send information, or a set of charges, through your blood and into your organs.

If the sound-based information being distributed through the phonons is positive and uplifting, the body remains in or achieves a greater state of health. If the sound-based data is negative or depressing, the body falls into a worsened state. Positive sounds are created by optimistic thoughts, songs, or noises, such as those produced through meditative chants, positive intention statements, and spiritual truths. Negative thinking and sounds are formed from pessimistic or downtrodden ways of thinking (Kshatri 2015).

As suggested by the phonon research, much of our mental and physical health is dependent on the sounds we don't always know we are hearing. In fact, the subtle energies of the body—and the world—far outnumber the physical energies. Russian physicist Yury Kronn has suggested that 96 percent of our existence is subtle, but we are not currently able to measure it (Kshatri 2016).

Given that there are so many subtle sounds affecting and being produced by us, it's imperative to find a way to supervise this subtle soup. It's not as difficult to direct subtle sound energies as you might think. You simply need to mindfully manage your subtle energy anatomy, which are the structures that govern your subtle energies and also many capacities of your physical anatomy.

Your Subtle Energy Anatomy

There are three main structures in the subtle energy anatomy. These are the *chakras*, or energy centers; *auric fields*, or bands of energy generated by the chakras; and *energy channels*, which flow through the body. For the purpose of developing our clairaudience and managing the subtle energies of sound, here we are primarily concerned with the chakras and auric fields.

Chakras are energy organs that lie inside or right around your body. Each of the seven in-body chakras are secured in the spine, associated with an endocrine gland, and regulate a specific set of physical, psychological, and spiritual concerns. (I also work with five out-of-body chakras, which were featured in my first book in this series. I'll touch on a couple of these chakras in later chapters, but I find it far simpler to teach clairaudience using the seven in-body chakras, as clairaudience is so frequently a body-based endeavor.) While each chakra has thousands of jobs, their main function is simple. Chakras convert subtle energy into physical energy and vice versa.

How can chakras accomplish this goal? Every chakra emanates and operates on a unique band of electromagnetic activity and sound. This means that each chakra can be described as a range of colors and tones. In turn, every chakra generates a corresponding auric field, which lies outside of the body and is encoded with the same frequencies as its chakra partner.

The auric fields add up to an overarching auric field. The individual fields, which are also called auric layers, play a critical role in the actualization of clairaudient sounds, if not all mystical phenomena. This is because every auric field serves as an energy filter.

Based on a complex set of programs, an auric field decides what subtle energies to either reject or let in to the subtle and physical anatomies. Every field accomplishes this job for a related section of the body as well as its correlated chakra. Basically, when a psychic missive connects with the overall auric field, it is assessed by the field that resonates with its frequency. This field then rebuffs or takes in the subtle message.

Acceptable subtle messages are allowed into matching areas of the body but are also absorbed by the chakra related to the external field. This chakra then sends the psychic data through our spine and other channels, such as the meridians, to be received by our brain. In turn, the brain interprets this subtle message and decides how to react.

How does the brain know what to do with the psychic input? It all depends on the chakra that shared the data.

Every chakra and related auric field governs a specific set of psychic or mystical functions, in addition to performing other tasks. As shown on figure 1 on the following page, the first chakra, located in the hip, attunes to physically empathic information. The sixth chakra, in the brow, is visual in orientation. And the fifth chakra, in the throat area, is the home of verbal communication.

If the brain has received a communication that entered through the visually oriented field and chakra, it will understand the subtle message in visual terms. In turn, the brain will present a visual picture in our mind, which is the basis of clairvoyance. If the dispatch is sensory, the brain will help us feel or sense a response. This is the heart of clairempathy, which relates through several chakras. And if the message enters through the fifth chakra, the home of verbal psychism, we hear a sound.

There are many processes through which the fifth chakra receives and shares psychic sounds. First of all, we must acknowledge the fact that the fifth chakra relates to the mouth, jaw, and ears. This means that our fifth chakra is complicit in physical hearing. When your ears hear a sound, your fifth chakra also resonates with that sound. And when sound waves are passed through the body and bones, they naturally affect your fifth chakra. Your fifth chakra, which is able to convert physical energy into psychic energy, can

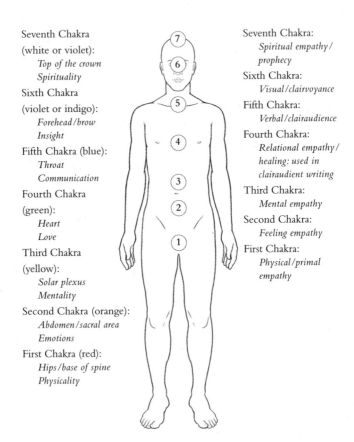

Seventh Chakra (white or violet):
Top of the crown
Spirituality

Sixth Chakra (violet or indigo):
Forehead/brow
Insight

Fifth Chakra (blue):
Throat
Communication

Fourth Chakra (green):
Heart
Love

Third Chakra (yellow):
Solar plexus
Mentality

Second Chakra (orange):
Abdomen/sacral area
Emotions

First Chakra (red):
Hips/base of spine
Physicality

Seventh Chakra:
Spiritual empathy/ prophecy

Sixth Chakra:
Visual/clairvoyance

Fifth Chakra:
Verbal/clairaudience

Fourth Chakra:
Relational empathy/ healing: used in clairaudient writing

Third Chakra:
Mental empathy

Second Chakra:
Feeling empathy

First Chakra:
Physical/primal empathy

FIGURE 1: *The Chakras and Their Psychic Skills*

unearth the psychic nugget from the physical noise and employ the brain to decipher that psychic dispatch.

As well, there are two sides to the fifth chakra, and to all in-body chakras, in fact. In general, the chakric backsides, which flow outward from the backside spine, usher in psychic data. That data is then processed in the center of a chakra, which shares it with other chakras. A psychic communiqué also makes its way to the brain, which interprets it. In turn, the front sides of all chakras, which extend frontward from the spine, express our brain's responses into the world. For instance, if a psychic message like "Watch out!" is sent via the fifth chakra's backside to the brain, the brain might relay a response to the front side of the chakra. We might yell "Why?" However, the brain can also send a demand to the first chakra, which manages physical functions. We just might leap to the side and thus save ourselves from an accident.

This interplay of the chakras, as well as the relationship between our subtle and physical anatomies, actually explains why we have six different forms of clairaudience. While the fifth chakra and brain are always involved in the receiving, decoding, and sharing of physical and subtle sounds, only one type of clairaudience always employs only the fifth chakra. In the case of the other five types of clairaudience, other chakras also join in the dance. This shouldn't be a surprise. Subtle energy is shareable across all chakras and through them, amongst all structures of the physical anatomy. Which chakras and their related fields are involved with which of the six forms of clairaudience? Let's take a look.

CLAIRAUDIENT FORM	ASSOCIATED CHAKRAS
Classical Clairaudience	Fifth chakra
Speaking in Tongues	Fifth and sometimes also the seventh chakra
Clairaudient Writing	Fifth and fourth chakras
Telepathic Empathy	Fifth chakra along with the following:
	Primal Telepathy: First chakra *Feeling Telepathy: Second chakra* *Mental Telepathy: Third chakra* *Spiritual Telepathy: Seventh chakra; can also employ sixth chakra*
Natural Clairaudience	Fifth chakra; also the eighth and tenth (the latter two chakras are explained in chapter 7)
Healing and Manifesting	Fifth and fourth chakras, among others

• • •

Now that you know the basics about clairaudience, it's time to pack your clairaudient tool kit full of even more concepts—and, more importantly, hands-on techniques.

● ● ● ● ● ●

Summary

Clairaudience is a mystical gift that involves the receiving and sending of auditory messages that are psychic in nature, whether the message is beyond the range of hearing or packaged within a normal sound. As a faculty, clairaudience has served humanity throughout time and is alive and well today.

To prepare you to further awaken your own clairaudience, this chapter outlined six basic types of clairaudience: classical clairaudience, speaking in tongues, clairaudient writing, telepathic empathy, natural clairaudience, and the use of clairaudience in healing and manifesting. These aptitudes are available to you because clairaudience is an energetic process, with energy being defined as "information that moves." As an energetic being, you employ physical and subtle structures that work together to form clairaudient experiences. Respectively, these structures are your ears, bones, skin, and central nervous system, as well as the chakras and auric fields. Both your physical and subtle selves interact to open you to the divine "ear" that is your clairaudience.

CHAPTER TWO

● ● ● ●

The Clairaudient's Toolkit

CONCEPTS AND TECHNIQUES

To be an expert at anything, you must understand the most pertinent concepts and acquire practical tools. The purpose of this chapter is to provide you with both. By the time you're finished with this chapter, you'll be on your way to developing your divine ear, one of the terms that refers to clairaudience. You'll also be ready to learn the specifics related to the six types of clairaudience, which you'll start doing in chapter 3.

Up front, I'll discuss and then show you the two most fundamental techniques necessary to conduct clairaudience. Called Spirit-to-Spirit and Healing Streams of Grace, these processes assure everything from energetic protection to accurate interpretations. I'll next walk you through two add-on exercises and a conversation about the need for safety during clairaudient activities.

I'll then jump into a few of the factors involved in awakening and strengthening your clairaudience. First I'll describe a few of the signs that might clue you in to an activating clairaudient gift. I'll then explore the various types of sources you can tap into and ways that negative sources can attach to you or affect you.

This latter topic leads directly into another important one: How do you distinguish between what clairaudience is and what it isn't? Maybe a voice is just a voice—or something else. After delving into this meaty topic, I'll help you better understand some of the dangers involved in clairaudience and depict a few of the symptoms that might indicate unhealthy clairaudience activity. Then I'll provide an exercise for securing a clairaudience guardian, one that will guarantee safe interactions. Lastly I'll turn to more creative matters, examining a few of the stones and tones that can be integrated into a clairaudience practice to bolster your effectiveness.

At the end of the chapter, I'll package the information here as questions to help you qualify or analyze a clairaudient interaction. I'll continue to add to this list of qualifiers at the end of all following chapters. All chapter questions will be collected and collated into appendix A at the end of the book for easy reference. Appendix B will provide a quick reference for performing the two main techniques used in this book, Spirit-to-Spirit and Healing Streams of Grace, which we'll cover in detail now.

Technique One
SPIRIT-TO-SPIRIT

Spirit-to-Spirit is my favorite technique. It's a three-step process that I developed years ago to accomplish several purposes. It keeps out harmful sources, guarantees the most accurate assessment of a clairaudient insight, assures that your own needs are respected when you're helping others, and encourages the best outcome for all concerned. Better yet, you can use this technique for yourself, someone else, or when interacting with a group. You can also employ it to seek out a clairaudient message or to check out a previously received communication. You can even use this process to send clairaudient-based information to someone else. In other words, Spirit-to-Spirit is an all-purpose activity.

Though I use the term "the Spirit" to describe the Oneness, employ whatever label you're comfortable with: Kwan Yin, Mary, Allah, the Christ, the Goddess, the Holy Spirit, God, the Universe, the Divine, the One, or even the Goodness in Humanity. I like using the label "the Spirit" because of my definition of a spirit.

Basically, a spirit is the essential and immortal aspect of a being that is alive or dead. This definition relates to people, animals, plants, star beings, and anything else that is conscious. When you put your personal spirit in charge of a clairaudient interaction, your truest self will manage the process. You accomplish this goal in step 1 of Spirit-to-Spirit by affirming the existence of your personal spirit.

Step 2 of Spirit-to-Spirit enables you to connect with the spiritual or highest aspects of others during a clairaudient activity. This statement applies to visible and invisible beings. That doesn't mean that someone or something else will respond by acting perfectly. It means that the most perfect aspect of another will be available for your clairaudient interaction.

What if you're undertaking a clairaudient activity when alone and you want spiritual assistance? Step 2 has you covered. Step 2 involves recognizing the highest aspect of any invisible beings that are present. Only those serving the utmost good can remain. If there are darker energies present, these will either flee or become apparent so you can deal with them. You'll use the ideas and techniques taught in this chapter to do the latter.

Step 3 of Spirit-to-Spirit turns your will and clairaudient process over to the Spirit. The Spirit will now illuminate only the messages supportive of the true selves of all involved, as well as establish boundaries between you and others. What more could you want?

In a nutshell, the three steps of Spirit-to-Spirit are as follows:

STEP 1: **Affirm Your Personal Spirit.** This step can be accomplished with a simple in-breath and the sensing of your immortal self. You can also compose an image, symbol, or sound representing your spirit and employ it every time you perform this step.

STEP 2: **Affirm Others' Spirits.** As with the previous step, sense the goodness in others or formulate a symbol, sense, or sound that portrays others as their highest selves.

STEP 3: **Affirm the Spirit.** Is there an image that will help you recognize the Spirit, such as a certain tone, mantra, or sound? Choose one that is meaningful to you.

It's now time to try out Spirit-to-Spirit.

Awakening Your Clairaudience
THROUGH SPIRIT-TO-SPIRIT

No matter how developed your clairaudient gift, there is more to awaken. In this exercise you'll engage Spirit-to-Spirit to practice the technique and also attune your fifth chakra, the main clairaudience energy center. Trust whatever you hear, and enjoy the process.

STEP 1: **Perform Spirit-to-Spirit.** Acknowledge your essential spirit, the spirits of your invisible helpers, and the Spirit.

STEP 2: **Focus on Your Fifth Chakra.** Your fifth chakra encompasses the front and backside of your throat area. Center your attention in the middle of this region and breathe deeply.

STEP 3: **Ask for Attunement.** Request that the Spirit emanate a sound that will completely attune this chakra for a high level of performance. This sound, which might be a word, song, message, chant, mantra, tone, or bit of poetry, will vibrate within your fifth chakra. The resonance will pave the way for further clairaudient activities. At this time, simply listen to this sound within your mind. If you want, express it verbally.

STEP 4: **Close.** Once this center feels cleansed and attuned, take a few breaths and return to your everyday life.

• • •

Spirit-to-Spirit is perfect partnered with the next exercise, Healing Streams of Grace. Healing Streams of Grace is a multipurpose process for delivering healing, enabling manifestation, clearing negative connections, and supporting loving outcomes. Comprehending the importance of this technique starts with knowing that the Spirit generates continual waves of grace, which is love that creates positive change.

Other names for the Healing Streams of Grace are "the streams," "healing streams," and "streams of grace." I view them as arms of light emanating from a star. The star is the Spirit, and the beaming streams are extensions of the Spirit's love. These are always available and customize themselves to someone's need. If a healing stream attaches to you or someone else, it will deliver the exact energy needed and alter in vibration until it is no longer required. It will then fall away.

I use healing streams to surround myself with protection, encompass or release a negative entity, transform empathic messages into auditory understandings, package a healing, attract a manifestation, and so much more. You'll practice these and other important applications in chapters 3 through 8.

As you connect with the streams in the following exercise, you'll notice that the process begins with Spirit-to-Spirit. You'll kick off every exercise or procedure in this book with Spirit-to-Spirit, which lays the foundation for safe and amplified clairaudient activity. In fact, I recommend that you always employ Spirit-to-Spirit when undertaking clairaudience, as it affords every protection and interpretive element needed.

Establishing Safety

WITH HEALING STREAMS OF GRACE

In this exercise you'll be bolstering your energetic parameters. You can use this exercise anytime you want to assure secure boundaries when practicing clairaudience.

STEP 1: **Perform Spirit-to-Spirit.** Acknowledge your essential self, others' spirits, and the Spirit.

STEP 2: **Request a Boundary.** Ask the Spirit to wrap you in healing streams. You might picture streams of various colors surrounding you. You might also feel a sun-like warmth encompassing you. Ask the Spirit to employ these streams to cleanse your individual auric fields while filling in holes, pockmarks, and slashes. After a time, notice that the Spirit weaves these separate fields into a unified cocoon of love.

STEP 3: **Hear the Song.** Inside the cocoon, ask the Spirit to sing you a "song of safety." This is a personalized composition made of frequencies that match your true self. You might literally hear a song or a set of tones, notes, or chants, or simply feel the resonance of the Spirit's love. These sounds will penetrate your body and chakras and fill in your auric field.

STEP 4: **Close.** When you feel completely secure, thank the Spirit and return to your everyday awareness.

Listening Specifics
FACTORS INVOLVED IN CLAIRAUDIENCE

Before you can wholeheartedly awaken and expand your clairaudience, it's vital to understand the various factors involved in using it. Covered in this section are several topics, including:

- signs indicating an awakening or active clairaudient gift;
- sources of clairaudient information; and
- "energetic attachments," subtle energy bonds that create negative clairaudient experiences.

As I discuss each of these areas, pay attention to your thoughts. Have you experienced a clairaudient stirring?

What sources are already connected to you? Do you believe you're affected by a negative being? You'll learn how to assess and release any negative sources after I review these topics.

Signs of an Awakening or Active Clairaudient Gift

Are you already using your clairaudience or does it seem flat? And maybe, just maybe, you're sensing a stirring or an increase in your ability. There are specific signs that indicate an awakening or changing clairaudient gift.

These signs usually strike when someone's clairaudience has been dormant or plateaued and it is time for takeoff. Clairaudience is ever-changing. As already discussed, some people have enjoyed or employed their clairaudience for as long as they can remember. More commonly a person senses a clairaudient ability much like hearing a far-off tone. You can almost make it out, and then suddenly—boom! Another common situation involves the sudden surge of an already-present clairaudient ability. This can occur when a low-grade gift shifts into high gear.

There are many reasons that your clairaudience can turn on or up. These include a crisis, transition, the furthering of your spiritual purpose, a romantic entanglement, increased training—or reading a book about the topic, such as this one.

I'll give you an example of how fluid clairaudience can be and why it's important to recognize the wake-up calls after sharing the list of signs, which might be heard internally or externally:

- sound of footsteps, doors slamming, or objects falling
- a voice calling your name
- whispering from a distinct voice that isn't your own
- sense of spirits around you
- inspiration coming through your writing
- sudden awareness of a profound truth
- hearing music that no one else hears
- ringing or buzzing in ears that isn't tinnitus
- conversation in your head between yourself and another voice
- presence of "imaginary" friends
- hearing of messages from animals, plants, stars, and the like
- perception of messages in literature that others don't perceive
- spotting of messages in songs, on the radio, or in others' conversations

- need for quiet—you hear "too
  much" and want to pull in

At varying times, I've experienced every one of these signs since I was a child. I've even had my clairaudience turn off and then back on. In fact, my clairaudience, which was active during childhood, closed when I was a teenager. There is a long story behind that statement; however, the short version is that I was so mad at God for hardships in my family life that I decided to stop being psychic. *Voilà*, no mystical abilities. My clairaudience awakened again—quite literally with a bang—in my early twenties, after I'd started therapy.

At about age twenty-two, I heard a voice call my name and a door crash. There wasn't a "real" door slamming, nor was there anyone in the house with me. Rather, my guides were reawakening my gift. Then, in my thirties, my clairaudience ceased again. I didn't know why at the time. Looking back, I think it's because I had to further develop my clairempathy and clairvoyance. Those gifts became very strong during that decade.

When I turned forty, I was roused one night by a knock on the door. I got up. There was no one there. Voices started whispering in my head, telling me that I was ready to talk with my "invisible community." Soon after, my clairaudient abilities once more opened. I began hearing my own and others' spiritual guides. I could also channel spiritual poetry and understand the language of many natural beings, including some of my pets.

Of course, the occurrence I've shared in the list of what can be an awakening clairaudient gift may not always be psychic. For example, I used to think that spirits were flitting in and out of my front door, leaving it ajar, until I figured out that Honey, my golden retriever, was unlocking the door with his nose. He would then run around outside before returning to his place on the couch. Go figure.

One of the most important ways to figure out if noises are clairaudient or not is to track them to their origin. This statement applies to all psychic sounds, whether they are obviously subtle or packaged within environmental noises. This activity is called sourcing. Understanding the concept of sourcing, and also how to perform it, is the backbone of clairaudience.

Sources, Sources, and More Sources

Sourcing is the verb I use to describe the act of figuring out the source of a psychic or environmental noise. Once you've determined if a sound is indeed clairaudient in nature or contains a nugget of mystical information, you can then track the message to the particular source or origin and qualify it. I use the word *qualify* to describe the process involved in assessing the integrity and applicability of a source. Is it a beneficial source? An informed source? Should you pay attention to it or not? These are the kinds of questions we ask when we are qualifying a source.

Qualifying a source is based on an important assumption, which is this: we get to decide who to listen to or talk with—or not. We don't deserve to be victimized by sources, visible or invisible, that are harmful or annoying. Throughout this book you'll be practicing ways to dismiss unhelpful sources.

As per the possible sources you can tap into, there are endless numbers of clairaudient sources existing on this plane and others. On any given day I might attune to a spiritual guide offering insight, a client's angelic guardian, an aspect of myself (such as an inner child or wise self), my dog Honey (Lucky, the lab, is quieter), my deceased father (who loves to visit), or a negative entity connected to a client. I might also hear a woodpecker telling me to take advantage of an opportunity or converse with a deceased relative in a dream.

The forms of clairaudient sounds can be as varied as their sources. An invisible guide might whisper in my ear, my client's angel might speak as if in the room, my inner self might replay a conversation I had in the past, and a negative entity might state unkind things aloud about a client. Know that sources can sing, hum, scream, shout, chant, or perform just about any other vocalization to get your attention.

Keeping in mind the range of sounds indicating a clairaudient experience, there are two main categories of sources:

WORLDLY: This grouping includes beings from this planet, whether they are earthly or fantastical, that might be living or deceased. Earthly members of this grouping include living and deceased people and natural beings, including animals and plants, but also aspects of any of these beings. For instance, you can connect with part of a person's soul or even an aspect of a plant's soul. Fantastical worldly beings include fairies, unicorns, or other mystical figures.

OTHERWORLDLY: This grouping involves beings from dimensions other than the third and from other planes of existence. This category includes angels, demons, and beings from other planets.

Sometimes it's hard to distinguish between a worldly or otherworldly source. What if a deceased friend shows up and tells you that he was once an angel—or has transformed into an interplanetary master? Maybe you were once a fairy in a past life, which means that your soul is simultaneously earthly and fantastical. My advice is to not get to worried about the specifics. What's most important is to decide if a source is Spirit-approved or not.

Spirit-approved sources are exactly that. If the Spirit nods its approval, the source is safe and informative. Non-Spirit-approved sources don't align with your spirit or your current needs and might even be dangerous. You'll learn more about these distinctions in the section "Sound Specifics" beginning on page 112.

Even a really "good" being might be bad for you. Years ago I participated in a ceremony in Peru. I was surrounded by men. A voice told all the men in the group that I should marry a certain group member. I didn't hear the voice, though, and the message felt wrong to me. The next day I used Spirit-to-Spirit to ask if that marching order was divinely approved. I immediately heard a no. My assumption was that a part of the would-be fiancé's personality was influencing the other group members.

Some sources are just plain bad, however. They might be dead or alive, worldly or otherworldly. Usually people call these sources *dark entities*. The term *entity*, however, refers to anything or anyone with a soul. The word *dark* connotes the entity's manipulative nature and its intent to steal a victim's positive energy, project its negative energy into a victim, or control a victim for personal gain. These dark entities can also be called interference or dark forces, and I'll discuss them further in the next section.

What determines which sources show up during a clairaudient activity? We all have at least two lifetime spiritual guides, which communicate the most frequently. Sources can also be situation-specific, revealing themselves to answer a certain question. They might also connect with us during the span of a project or to assist with a goal, and then disappear. However, beings will frequently connect because they match you energetically. For instance, if you've been a fairy in a past life, you'll probably attract a lot of fairy guides. Other factors that influence which specific beings link with you include the following:

- genetic influence and ancestry
- soul and past life experiences
- destiny—choices made by your soul and spirit
- family-of-origin modeling and programming
- life experiences, positive and negative
- cultural standards and beliefs

- religious beliefs
- your personality
- divine intervention

As an example, you'll more likely attract an ancestor from your family line than one from someone else's. If your personality is bubbly, you might appeal to more optimistic sources.

There are reasons that we might attract dark forces as well, a subject we'll explore next.

Negative Entities, Attachments, and Challenges

Hearing negative entities doesn't mean that you're bad. Darker forces exist, which makes it likely that you've already heard from them and will again.

As shared in the last section, negative entities have two main goals in mind when they intrude in someone's life: they want to steal another's energy or project their own problematic energy onto others. Basically, they are irresponsible. They don't want to go to the Spirit for nourishment and assistance or deal with their own deeper issues. To avoid their own pain, they often attack, attach, and manipulate other people or beings. They select victims whose issues make them vulnerable. What makes you susceptible to interference? Return to the list offered in the previous section, which includes everything from child-hood abuse to genetic programming.

What might interference appear, sound, or feel like? There are thousands of permutations, but one example relates to a client I once worked with who was taunted in her dreams by her dead grandmother. The grandmother would call my client names and was especially caustic about my client's sex life. In the dreams the grandmother's face was angry and pinched, and my client always felt shameful.

Working together, my client and I figured out that the grandmother was stuck between this world and the heavens, scared that "the Maker" would judge her for having a child—my client's mother—out of wedlock. Basically, the grandmother was trying to dump her shame on the granddaughter. With my help, my client conversed with her grandmother's soul. She reassured her grandmother, telling her that God would forgive her for the sexual "sin." My client sensed that her grandmother felt relieved. The grandmother whispered "thank you" in such a way that I could hear the voice as well. The grandmother stopped visiting.

In this example, the granddaughter was vulnerable to interference because she was related to the intruding soul.

She'd only been plagued by her grandmother for about a year, however, ever since her grandmother had died. Some disturbing relationships can be more long-term. These usually involve contractual arrangements formed by subtle energy attachments.

Attachments are unnatural and unhealthy bonds initiated through a conscious or unconscious agreement between individuals or groups comprised of people, natural beings, or supernatural entities. They are always negative and form limiting relationships, determining what energy can be exchanged or not between members of what becomes an energy contract, which is enforced through a subtle attachment. These attachments, which look like ropes, bonds, wires, or other forms of linkage, can connect beings through their subtle energy structures or their souls.

Even if one or both of the original contract holders dies, the attachment might continue until it's released. Thus, this bond can tie souls or groups together lifetime after lifetime. Even if one contract member finally escapes the binding, the other contractual member/s remain vulnerable to re-creating a similar association, just with a different being.

While a member of a subtle contract remains connected to the original co-signer/s until they sign off, they also form the same type of attachment with others. Like attracts like. For example, imagine you unconsciously created a subtle attachment with your mother when in utero. The contractual agreement was that you'd give her your life energy and she'd deposit her negative emotions in you. What do you gain? Survival. Guess what? Later in life you'll attract individuals who project their emotions onto you and steal your vital energy. The pattern established with your mother basically becomes a gift that keeps on giving.

There are other energetic challenges that can draw the interest of negative entities. These are wounds in the subtle structures. A cruel voice can slash your auric field, leaving a gaping hole through which negative entities can project their energies. A mean statement can damage a chakra, creating a soft spot for a dark force to pull energy from.

As you read through the types of attachments and injuries that a negative source can cause or exploit, pay attention to your intuition. Does any item on the list strike you as being already present? You can heal it through the exercise that follows.

ENERGY INFLUENCE	DESCRIPTION
Cord/s	A cord is an unhealthy energetic attachment. It psychically appears like a garden hose and interlocks two or more beings, limiting both.
Curse	A curse is an energetic device that psychically looks like a mess of cords. It is programmed to attract certain types of negativity to the accursed.
Slashes	Slashes appear psychically like knife wounds that cause a seepage of healthy energy and an intrusion from toxic energies.
Holes and Leaks	There are other types of problems that trauma or negative entities can create or manipulate through. Negative interactions form holes, leaks, puncture wounds, gaps, or other issues in the auric field or chakras.

• • •

By far the easiest way to manage sources and decrease your susceptibility to negative entities is to make sure a source is positive, and if it isn't, to clear attachments and repair wounds. The following exercise will help you accomplish both goals.

Exercise
--3--

Assessing a Clairaudient Source

CLEARING ENERGETIC
ATTACHMENTS AND WOUNDS

This simple exercise will help you track a questionable source, release attachments, and fix energetic wounds. It also can be undertaken if you are aware of a questionable clairaudient source or just want to double-check one that has shown up.

If you're already involved in a clairaudient activity, you can insert this exercise at any time to evaluate for negative energies and release them. Simply jump into step 2, walk through the remainder of the exercise, and return to your clairaudient activity, having been cleansed of the unhealthy energetics.

STEP 1: **Conduct Spirit-to-Spirit.** Acknowledge your personal spirit, others' spirits, and the Spirit.

STEP 2: **Assess for Negative Energetics.** How do you know if something negative is influencing you? Following are a few indications:

- *Negative Beings:* Negative influences will smell bad, make you feel really hot, cold, or uncomfortable, or cause you to feel disturbed, dissociated, heavy, or full of trepidation. You might perceive them psychically as gray, cloudy, or black in coloration, and they will sound manipulative or bossy. Other indications are covered in this and later chapters.

- *Attachments or Injuries:* Reference the psychic descriptions covered earlier in this chapter to psychically see attachments and energetic wounds. From a sensory point of view, the subtle or physical areas around attachments or injuries will feel bogged down and oversaturated, empty and thin, or painful and inflamed. Problematic areas will have a different tonal quality than healthy areas, and sometimes you can hear a hiss where energy is leaking into or out of the subtle or physical system.

STEP 3: **Pinpoint the Negative Source.** In a meditative state, ask the Spirit to provide a clairaudient message, such as a sound, word, tone, or noise, to describe the source that has caused an attachment or wounded area. You might also psychically see or sense this source. Even energetic injuries are caused by interactions. Remain focused on this step until you have a strong sense of the harmful source.

STEP 4: **Contain and Release the Negative Influence.** Ask the Spirit to surround the harmful source in healing streams and to bring it to a place of love and safety, thus releasing you and any other beings affected by its influence. It's beneficial to ask the Spirit why this interference engaged with you. How has it been benefiting from your association? Did you perceive it was meeting a need for you? Most importantly, ask the Spirit to tell or show you a better way to meet that need.

STEP 5: **Surrender Energetic Attachments.** If there are energetic attachments or wounds, request that the Spirit send healing streams of grace through them. These will disintegrate the attachments or heal the wounds and replace what's been causing harm with love.

STEP 6: **Close.** Thank all the beings who helped in this process. Commit to reflecting on any lessons learned from your association with the negative influence, and return to your regular life when ready.

Additional Points for Discernment

You can hear subtle sounds that aren't clairaudient. Rather, they might be caused by any of the following:

- **Repetition of Abuse:** Trauma can mask itself as a clairaudient event. The bothersome voice in the head or psychically loud tone might be a leftover from the past. Professional assistance can help you determine if an auditory event is psychic or psychological.

- **Fantasy:** Humans are imaginative beings. We make up situations and predict outcomes so we can make informed choices. But we can also confuse an imagined message with true clairaudient input. The litmus test? If you can alter an auditory message—maybe move the words around with your mind—you're probably dealing with a fantasy. Genuine clairaudient messages can't be retooled.

- **Others' Energies:** Everyone and everything emanates energy. Think of how much energy, physical and psychic, surrounds you at any given time. It's easy to confuse another's energy with your own. Is that radio song meant for you or another passenger in the car? Is that psychic voice directed at you or a family member? Use Spirit-to-Spirit to clarify the true recipient of a clairaudient sound and Healing Streams of Grace to release those not meant for you.

- **Mental Challenges:** Various medical and psychiatric professionals assert that hearing sounds or voices is an indication of mental illness. In fact, auditory verbal hallucinations (AVH) are a component of many psychological conditions, such as schizophrenia and border-line personality disorder. Because of this, it's important to get professional input if you hear startling and menacing voices. Only a professional can really help you figure out what's going on.

There do seem to be particular indicators, however, that differentiate AVH from clairaudient experiences. As a backgrounder, a paper by the Royal College of Psychiatrists analyzed 25 individuals who heard voices, internally or externally. These voices seemed to emanate from entities that were controlling, bossy, and intrusive. In general, the researchers could only diagnose a psychiatric condition when the voices stimulated increased activities in two specific sections of the brain or altered the dopamine synthesis. In fact, they acknowledged that AVH occurs in up to 20 percent of healthy people who aren't psychotic (Upthegrove 2016).

What this means is that clairaudient sounds can indicate mental illness or stress, but not necessarily so. In my own practice, I make sure that anyone persistently bothered by voices work with a psychologist or psychiatrist. In turn, if the professional also wants them to work with me, I will. We are all psychic but also physical and need to employ all means available to create a balanced life.

While the above list suggests events that might be confused with clairaudience, there are indicators of another common issue, which involves being plagued by a too-active clairaudient ability. I'll cover this topic next.

The Overly Psychic Clairaudient

RED FLAGS AND WARNING SIGNS

Years ago I worked with a young woman named Angel. She had been clairaudient her entire life but had never developed boundaries. She heard whispers several times during the day and night. Sometimes she could distinguish between them—a deceased ancestor, a ghost, a demon—but she could never turn off the spigot. And sometimes these beings entered her body.

When they did, they often requested healing. Angel sensed that they used her vital energy to improve themselves, as she felt drained when they were inside. She also felt hot, flushed, and sick. After a being exited, she would be chilled and exhausted for hours, another indication that they had siphoned her life energy. When I asked Angel why she let the entities enter her body, she seemed puzzled.

"Well, if I'm capable of helping them, God would want me to," she explained.

I sensed that there was more to the story, so I asked Angel if she really believed that God would want her to self-sacrifice or if there was a deeper reason she engaged with these beings. Angel started to cry.

"No one talked to me when I was growing up but the spirits," she shared. "They have been my only friends." Basically, Angel's parents ignored her. Her only friends were invisible, and her lack of social skills kept people at bay.

Angel had a rationale for being overly clairaudient, but it was making her unhappy and unhealthy. I taught Angel the exercise showcased later in this chapter, "Getting a Gatekeeper," and reduced her clairaudient contacts to a single source. I then surrounded her with healing streams and supported her in getting to know real people. Feeling less unusual, she started developing friendships, which rounded out her life.

I share this story—and I could dredge up thousands like it—to emphasize the importance of maintaining good boundaries when being clairaudient. But how do you know if you're too exposed or open, or if you're taking in too much of another's energy? There are long-term and short-term symptoms.

The immediate short-term symptoms of being hyper-clairaudient include the following:

- rapid or arrhythmic heartbeat
- instant sweating

- intense heat, numbness, or chill
- feeling faint
- the sense that something is wrong
- dissociation—the inability to connect with your body
- tingling (where entity or attachment is connecting)
- nausea and flu-like symptoms
- reddened or flushed skin
- a blackout
- sound of rushing water
- sense of being in a tunnel
- muscular weakness
- skin sensitivity

I experienced many of these symptoms the first time a deceased person—a ghost—attempted to enter my body. I was taking a psychic development class. The teacher had told us to channel a dead person. She didn't teach us about boundaries or how to qualify the source. She just told us to let a deceased soul into our body so we could talk with it.

Immediately I felt a hot flush on my neck and a prickling sensation. A foggy energy started creeping into my body. Sick to my stomach and freezing cold, I felt like the incoming entity was trying to push my soul out of my body. Desperate, I asked this being who it was.

"Tom," a voice said in my head. "I'm Tom the sailor."

I angrily demanded that Tom the sailor leave me alone. I figured he could get his own body instead of overtaking mine. It took me hours to still my racing heart and recover physically and emotionally. That lesson taught me the importance of boundaries in regard to our clairaudient rights. We don't have to connect with anything or anyone we don't want to—and we certainly don't have to let something into our body.

That experience also prompted me to assess myself and others for not only the short-term signs of weak energetic boundaries but also indicators of a long-term hyperactive clairaudience. These include:

- weight gain, which can occur if your soul leaves your body too frequently; the body holds weight to feel safer
- build-up of toxins, psychic and physical
- loss of personal power (from being controlled by uninformed or manipulative sources)

- interference from an evil or misleading source
- garbling of messages—can't distinguish between accurate and incorrect information
- blurred line between yourself and an entity/entities
- mix-up between clairaudient and psychological information
- over-reliance on clairaudient sources; eventual inability to think for self
- loss of own energy due to sustaining another being or group of beings
- additional biochemical alterations to your body, such as hormonal imbalances and intense food cravings
- changes in sleep or sexual patterns
- awareness of memories that aren't your own
- grief resulting from loss of self

Obviously, many mental or physical conditions can cause the above symptoms. If you are performing verbal psychic functions, however, and experience any of the above situations, immediately stop using your clairaudience, ask for healing streams, and investigate for causes. I also recommend getting a gatekeeper.

A gatekeeper is a spiritual guardian that serves as your one and only psychic connection besides the Spirit. (The Spirit can also be your gatekeeper.) This invisible being helps you with a number of activities, including:

- filters sources
- only allows you to connect with helpful sources
- acts like a "watch dog" when you are interacting with other sources
- summons the sources needed for specific concerns
- regulates the flow of psychic information inside and outside of you
- helps you learn lessons in a gentle way
- protects you from harmful or unnecessary entities and information
- points out and helps you release harmful entities and attachments
- overrides you if you might harm yourself or someone else
- steadily serves the Spirit
- builds your self-esteem and capabilities

Now it's time to obtain a gatekeeper.

Exercise
—4—

Getting a Gatekeeper

The following exercise can be used to get a gatekeeper. Know that the Spirit can also serve as your gatekeeper, in which case this exercise will serve as a confirmation of that fact.

STEP 1: **Conduct Spirit-to-Spirit.** Affirm your personal spirit, others' spirits, and the Spirit.

STEP 2: **Request a Gatekeeper.** Directly ask the Spirit to send you a gatekeeper. You might instantly hear or see this gatekeeper or perceive it later in a dream or through a sign. You can become aware of the gatekeeper through any of your senses: feeling, smell, awareness, sight, and, of course, hearing.

STEP 3: **Greet the Gatekeeper.** Interact with the gatekeeper. Ask its name and why the Spirit appointed it. Ask it how you can best summon it and how you'll know it's present. Remain in process until you are able to receive a clairaudi-ent sensation from the gatekeeper: a word, voice, noise, memory of an auditory interaction, song, tone, chant, or another sound. As suggested, the Spirit might be your gatekeeper. If this is your sense, ask the Spirit to confirm this in a way you'll understand.

STEP 4: **Close in Gratitude.** Thank the gatekeeper for its kind and powerful help, and return to your everyday life when ready.

And for the Creative You...
STONES AND TONES

Stones and tones have been used for thousands of years to amplify clairaudient capabilities. Keep the following information in mind for all clairaudient encounters. I'll refer to this information periodically throughout this book.

Stones for Clairaudience

The most classic clairaudient image across time is of a medium sitting at a table while conducting a séance with a crystal ball on the table. The crystal ball isn't actually an intercom. It's a tool for focusing, and there are many types of stones that bolster clairaudience.

How do you work with a stone? There are dozens of ways. You can hold a stone, wear it as jewelry, put a tiny one in a pocket, or set stones in your environment. You can actually employ a crystal ball if you want, staring at it while focusing your clairaudient intentions. Following are several of the most well-known of the clairaudient stones and how they can benefit your clairaudience.

BLUE KYANITE: Aligns and clears all the chakras to support your clairaudience.

BLUE TOURMALINE: Enhances mediumship.

DUMORTIERITE: Amplifies gifts; helps you speak for yourself.

IOLITE: Called the "stone of the muses," iolite helps you express creatively through clairaudience, such as when you're bringing through poetry and songs.

LABRADORITE: Shields you from negativity.

LAPIS LAZULI: Links you with guides and angels.

MOLDAVITE: A meteoric gemstone, moldavite heightens clairaudient experiences. It makes voices louder, songs more clear, etc.

TURQUOISE: Provides spiritual attunement and anchors energies from higher guides.

* * * *

Of these stones, my personal favorite is turquoise. I've been lucky to learn from Hopi, Navajo, Mayan, and other shamans who employ turquoise in their practices. In fact, a Native American friend of mine made me a beautiful turquoise necklace, which I wear when relying heavily on my clairaudience.

In the verbiage of the Pueblo Indians, such as the Hopis, turquoise assists us in connecting with the *kachinas*, immortal spirit beings that serve particular purposes. For instance, one kachina calls in the rain; another attracts the right housing. I believe that the kachinas are similar to the Catholic saints, Judeo-Christian-Islamic angels, and guides by any other name. If I need something for my everyday life, I hold or touch a turquoise stone, conduct Spirit-to-Spirit, and ask the Spirit to send me the appropriate kachina or guide to assist me with my endeavor. You might want to try the same.

Tones for Attunement

According to Hindu philosophy, every chakra contains a *bija,* or seed syllable—a sound that attunes and reflects that chakra. Clairaudience is greatly amplified when we internally or externally chant the bija, also called a mantra, related to the fifth chakra. The bija will also clear, clean, enhance, and protect its partnered chakra and field.

If performing clairaudience with a chakra in addition to the fifth, you can also chant that chakra's bija. String together as many chakric seed syllables as you desire, like a pianist playing a composition.

In fact, try it now. Close your eyes and concentrate on your fifth chakra while chanting the related syllable, which is pronounced as "hum." Then chant the seed syllables for chakras one through seven, starting with the first and working your way up. Repeat the fifth seed syllable after the fourth. End by returning to "hum."

Sense how clear you feel. This process is an ideal way to begin any clairaudient session or to clean yourself after one.

First chakra	Lam, pronounced "lum."
Second chakra	Vam, pronounced "vum."
Third chakra	Ram, pronounced "rum."
Fourth chakra	Yam, pronounced "yum."
Fifth chakra	Ham, pronounced "hum."
Sixth chakra	Om, pronounced with a long O sound.
Seventh chakra	No specific syllable. However, it is associated with two different breathing sounds: visarga (pronounced with a breathy "ahhh") and NG (which sounds like the end of the word *sing*).

Questions for Assessing a Clairaudient Communication

The following questions relate to the topics in this chapter and can be used to help assess or qualify a clairaudient experience. I'll present questions at the end of all subsequent chapters to build an exhaustive list for assessing clairaudient activities. All questions will be gathered in appendix A.

The following are chapter-specific questions:

- Is this sound internal or external or both?

- Is the sound primarily composed of any of the following?
    - a voice or voices
    - noise
    - environmental sounds
    - music
    - chanting
    - tones
    - other: ringing, buzzing, humming, slamming, animalistic, etc.

- Is this source...
    - ★ worldly?
        - *alive person/people, deceased person/people, natural being/s, the self, part of the self, part of another's self, fantastical*
    - ★ otherworldly?
    - ★ Spirit-approved?
    - ★ not Spirit-approved?
- Am I being affected by any of the following:
    - ★ energetic attachment?
        - *cord, curse*
    - ★ energetic wound?
- Should I be using my gatekeeper?
- Am I sure this message is clairaudient or is it...
    - ★ repetition of abuse?
    - ★ fantasy?
    - ★ others' energies?
    - ★ a mental challenge?
- Am I experiencing any clairaudient red flags?
    - ★ short-term
    - ★ long-term
- Would a stone assist my clairaudient process?
- Would seed syllables assist my clairaudient process?

• • • • • • •

Summary

In this chapter you acquired the ideas and practices needed to help you employ your clairaudience in a healthy manner. You learned the two basic techniques that you'll use over and over, Spirit-to-Spirit and Healing Streams of Grace, along with several other exercises. You then examined clairaudience from several points of view, were taught the signs of activating clairaudience, and were instructed in the various types of energetic sources and dangers. Finally, I described the stones and tones that can be used to cleanse, empower, and protect you during clairaudient activity—and we're just starting!

• • • •

CHAPTER THREE

Classical Clairaudience

Now that you've gathered an extensive toolkit, it's time to explore classical clairaudience, the most well-known of all the forms of clairaudience. You've heard the terms *medium* and *channel*? Well, this is the chapter that will teach you how to safely serve as a pass-through vehicle, medium, or channel for a source.

As we proceed, I'll discuss the three main types of classical clairaudience and share examples of each. After that, I'll explain the link between brain states and classical clairaudience, showing you how to access and shift between the three types of classical clairaudience by changing brain states.

Next I'll present several qualifiers to help you assess a source and interpret its message. We'll investigate how to analyze the qualities of a source and its sounds, as well as the meaning of your own feelings and bodily sensations. Part of this discussion will include a briefing on environmental sounds, which can convey their own meaning.

Then I'll gather this data into a channeling exercise, adding tips that will help you wisely develop all capacities of your classical clairaudient abilities. And what decent classical clairaudient text wouldn't show you how to conduct a séance? All this and more is contained within this chapter.

The Three Styles of Classical Clairaudience

What mystical message have you recently received, whether deliberately summoned or not, when awake, asleep, or in your everyday life? Classical clairaudience occurs when we channel or serve as a medium for a human source (including the living and the dead), an aspect of a human, or any other entity or group of entities, such as otherworldly sources like masters, angels, or demons. Basically, this form of clairaudience is the basis of all clairaudience methods that require connecting with a conscious being.

As a note, I'll cover the means for receiving messages from natural beings, including animals and plants as well as off-world beings, such as extraterrestrials, in chapter 7.

A further discussion of the three main types of channeling follows.

1: Full Mediumship/Channeling

When performing full mediumship, your soul leaves your body and another entity or group of entities enter. They then proceed to share verbal messages through your body. Most of the time, you will be unaware of the message coming to and through you until your soul has returned to your body.

Most of the potential dangers of clairaudience relate to this practice. Think of it: when someone else is running your body, you aren't.

I experienced a startling full transmediumship experience several years ago. A client brought her six-year-old son to see me. She was sure that he was a channel for a demon. In front of me, the young boy's face turned purple and he began to shriek, uttering profanities that a child that young wouldn't know. I agreed with her assessment. I used healing streams to surround the wayward invader that was occupying this poor boy's body. Then I asked Spirit to lift the dark force out of the child's body and permanently affix the child's soul in his own body. Both the mother and myself saw a purple cloud drift out of the room.

The boy sighed and then sleepily said that he'd been "locked outside of his body." He shared that when I was using the streams, an angel had brought him back into his body and assured him that he'd never have to leave it again.

Full transmediumship can be frightening, but also richly rewarding. As an example, I struggled with panic attacks for a couple of years. Although infrequent, they were challenging. Based on the Spirit's advice, I asked my future self, the one healed from the anxiety, to enter my body. My current self stepped out for a time. When I reentered by body—and stopped feeling dissociated—my body was completely calm. I've been much more serene since my future self "fixed" my neurological system, and I haven't had a single additional panic attack. You'll learn a similar technique in chapter 8.

Because of the intense impact that an incoming soul can have on a body, I'll share ways to assure more bodily ease when performing full mediumship later in this chapter.

2: Partial Mediumship / Channeling

When employing partial channeling, your soul shares your body with an incoming entity or group of entities. Because you're entirely present, you can assume at least limited control over the entity and offer directives as per the message coming through.

My favorite partial channeling experience occurred years ago, when the Archangel Michael entered my body during a session. While holding my soul in his wings, he directed a laser-like energy toward my client. She had never had a loving relationship because her father had died when she was young.

The client immediately began crying. Michael's blessing awakened the memories of her father's love and, with them, her heart. Her life improved dramatically afterward, and a few years later she called me, overjoyed. She was finally in an amazing romantic relationship. I believe that the Archangel Michael used my physical body to send the needed frequencies of love to my client. Not only did my client's life improve, I felt happier for days on end. In fact, upon refection, I'm sure that the reason Michael entered me, instead of directly interrelating with my client, was that I had long-term issues with my own father. While I knew that my father loved me, he also had addiction problems when I was growing up, leading me to question how deeply he could care for me. While Michael healed my client, he helped me with the equivalent issue. You could say that Michael was performing a "two-for-one" healing.

Some clients question the reason to perform partial channeling at all. Why not undertake full channeling or the safer receptive channeling? There are many reasons that partial channeling can be the best choice. As I experienced with Archangel Michael, you might gain helpful energy through the partial channeling interaction. As well, an incoming soul might need our assistance to deliver a message or healing to another person. Perhaps the source doesn't speak in a language understood by the final recipient of the message. In this case, that source might need to use your brain and vocal cords to be understood. And sometimes you might require the assistance of the incoming being to accomplish a personal goal. For instance, I have a client who insists that a deceased naturalist shares her body when she's gardening, making sure that she cares for the plants in the best possible way. As another example, I have a friend who is an artist. He frequently invites famous individuals into his physical body. They then describe what their lives were like via his clairaudient capability, and he paints what they are depicting.

As I have done with full transmediumship, I have also performed self-growth work via partial transmediumship. With a therapist guiding me, I brought my deceased grandparents' souls into my body, one at a time. While experiencing their lives through my own senses, I was able to forgive them for their errors. Long-held family resentments fell off me, freeing me from many negative patterns.

3: Receptive Mediumship/Channeling

Receptive channeling is by far the easiest and safest classical clairaudient activity. You remain in your body and everything else stays outside of it.

You can use receptive mediumship for nearly any reason. For example, when I needed to buy a new car a few years ago, my deceased father showed up in a dream. He insisted that I buy a Ford. That car has been the most stable one I've ever owned.

My father has also sent messages to me through others. A few years ago, I had a friend living with me who was quite mechanical. One day, he asked, "Who is Wally?"

"That was my dad's name," I answered. "Why?"

"That's the name of the spirit that keeps following me around, telling me what to fix in your house," he explained.

My father, Walter, did carpentry in his free time. Little wonder he was looking out after my house.

How do you know which form of classical clairaudience you might be using or should be using—or how to shift from one to another, if need be? Each of the styles relates to differing trance states, which are rooted in varying brain states. I can better make this point after educating you about brain states and brain waves.

Brain States for Clairaudience

Since time began, experts have understood that mystical data is most easily received and understood in a trance state. There are numerous trance states, which are often induced through activities including meditation, prayer, intention, the use of sacred medicine, and sometimes even a fever or illness. Overall, to enter a "shamanic trance," we must set aside our ego and be available to beings and energies from the various realms of existence.

The three main forms of classical clairaudience are each associated with different trance states, though these overlap. And the major trance states can be linked to the main brain states, which are themselves connected to brain waves. By asking the Spirit to shift you into a specific brain state, you can steer your classical clairaudient activity.

Brain waves are the electrical pulses created by the firing of nerves in the brain. They are also affected by electromagnetic activity elsewhere in the body, such as the heart. Brain wave speeds are measured in hertz, which are cycles per second, and are divided into bands of waves. The categories of these waves are usually listed from the most to the least active.

A brain state is a snapshot of the central nervous system. Technically, a brain state is produced by an explicit pattern of neurological firing and chemical interactions. A brain state can be composed of various brain waves but is most affected by a specific brain wave. Each brain state equates with a certain type of trance state.

Following is a chart that showcases the relationship between a specific brain wave and its related brain state. The name I use for the brain state also describes the type of awareness or trance you achieve through that state. Also outlined are the types of classical clairaudience that you can access through that state. After presenting this information, I'll present a quick exercise showing you how to consciously shift into each brain state. By undertaking this exercise, you'll also be learning how to slide into the desirable classical clairaudient style or move from one style into another.

BRAIN–WAVE (HERTZ)	LABEL FOR STATE	TYPE OF CLASSICAL CLAIRAUDIENCE
Gamma (25–100 Hz)	Hyper-spiritual	Partial, full
Beta (14–30 Hz)	Aware	Receptive
Alpha (8–14 Hz)	Expanded	Receptive
Theta (4–8 Hz)	Meditative	Partial
Delta (.5 to 4 Hz)	Sleep	Receptive, partial, full
Infra-low (.5 Hz and under)	Primal	Partial, full

DESCRIPTION

In gamma we operate totally spiritually, even while we're fully grounded. We can sense and know all things.

In beta we are fully aware of our bodies and feelings. We can pick up messages from the environment and entities but have to think about their meaning.

Alpha puts us in a light trance. The mind won't interfere with a clairaudient process, but we'll understand the meaning of all psychic messages.

In theta you are aware of your body but remain sensitive to all things spiritual. You can also change subtle energies into physical and vice versa, and also partner with beings that can do this for you.

Through delta, your soul can connect with other beings. This occurs whether your soul is in or out of your body; as well, the beings can enter the body or remain external. You enter delta through light or deep sleep.

Infra-low brain waves are associated with cortical rhythms, which record our deepest needs and stressors. Connect with sub-aspects of the self through partial channeling to discover and heal sources of trauma or bring another being in to create neurological change.

If you'd like to try out these states, the following short exercise will enable you to do just that.

Testing the Brain States

The following exercise will help you experience each brain state. In the process, you'll be learning how to move from one form of classical clairaudience to another.

STEP 1: **Conduct Spirit-to-Spirit.** Affirm your own spirit, others' spirits, and the Spirit.

STEP 2: **Experience Each Brain State.** Without plunging too deeply into each brain wave and corollary brain and trance state, allow the Spirit or your gatekeeper to drop you briefly into each of these levels of awareness.

- *Gamma/Hyper-Spiritual:* Sense your spirit reaching into the heavens even as it remains attuned to your body. You are in total oneness with self and all. Thusly interconnected, you understand that other beings are within you and you are within them. You can even step outside of your body and remain fully linked to the "All" while remaining completely individuated and self-aware.

- ***Beta/Aware:*** In this everyday state of awareness, breathe deeply and accept everything you sense and feel. If you wish, you can pick up on information from beings outside of yourself and use your mind to interpret them.

- ***Alpha/Expanded:*** Falling into a light trance, become aware of your body, your chakras, and your overall auric field. In this state you'll sense and feel any beings that are near you, and your mind will automatically understand the meaning of their spiritual messages.

- ***Theta/Meditative:*** Entering theta is like moving into the portal of light that is your heart. You can now draw a loving being into you and partner with it to create positive change.

- ***Delta/Sleep:*** Request that the Spirit keep you awake, even as you experience how your body feels when, perfectly rested, you are greeted by a messenger. You might be inside or outside of your body when this being brings you a gift of knowledge. The source either remains outside of you or enters to deliver this blessing.

- ***Infra-Low/Primal:*** The Spirit, in the form of the Divine Mother, helps you sense, see, or feel the neediest aspect of yourself. Then she cradles this primal self within waves of misty love. She sends into the oceanic cocoon all the love required to repair the twisted wires and broken parts of your neediest self. Then she hums a soft sound and you know that this primal self is finally experiencing true safety and security. In fact, she whispers that she can do this for you at any time.

STEP 3: **Close.** Let the Spirit guide you into your everyday senses. Return to your life when ready.

Sound Specifics
QUALIFYING THOSE VOICES

Now that you know about the states that enable different levels of classical clairaudience, it's time to learn more about evaluating a source and its message. Following are ways to analyze a source's viability and gain an interpretive edge by assessing its voice or sounds. The information in this section will help you decide if you want to work with a source and exactly how to interpret a valid message.

Analyzing a Source

What will help you figure out the nature and integrity of a source that's been presented? While some of the following ideas were presented earlier in this book, this section will deepen this material and present new data.

SPIRIT-APPROVED/NOT SPIRIT-APPROVED: Basically all sources are either Spirit-approved or not. In general, the main differences are these:

NOT SPIRIT-APPROVED	SPIRIT-APPROVED
Manipulates through shame or fear tactics	Decreases fear; sounds loving
Employs bigotry or manipulation	Employs facts
Decreases self-esteem; increases arrogance	Increases self-awareness; encourages growth
Discourages hard work	Encourages working toward potential
Demands worship of them, not the Spirit	Points the way to the Spirit
Encourages you to ignore obligations	Boosts your ability to fulfill responsibilities
Encourages you to benefit from another's demise	Encourages you to assist others and self

INTERNAL/EXTERNAL: As stated in previous chapters, internal voices are heard inside the mind and external voices enter through the ears or pass into the brain through the body. The location of the voice clues you in to the type of channeling. During full channeling, the source's voice is inside your body and your voice is outside. When performing partial channeling, the source's voice and your own are internal. During receptive channeling, your voice is internal and the source's voice remains external.

OWN VOICE/OTHER VOICE: Is the sound (or voice) you're hearing your own or another's? This differentiation will immediately tell you if you're dealing with an aspect of yourself or an outsider.

SINGLE SOURCE/PLURAL SOURCE: While most channeling involves a single source, there are souls that travel in a group. These might speak in unison or one at a time. One example is a set of dark forces called a *legion*. This collective is made of interconnected negative entities and is led by an even more evil spokesperson. Groups of positive beings can also journey as a crowd. For instance, angels journey in a group called a *flight*, which is usually headed by an archangel.

HUMAN/OTHERWORLDLY: A source can be human or an aspect of a human, such as an inner child, a wise self, or a part of the mind. It might also be otherworldly, including angels and demons. Nature-based sources also divide into groupings. One group is *earthly*. Within this listing, sources are normal or fantastical. Another group is *otherworldly*. This category includes beings indigenous to non-earth places, such as stars or other dimensions. Natural sources are dealt with in chapter 7.

ALIVE/DECEASED/OTHER: When performing classical channeling, it's helpful to figure out if you're connecting with a being (or part of a being) that is alive or deceased. You will alter your understanding of the message depending on this information. For instance, imagine that an ancestor from a thousand years ago shares a cooking recipe. You'll have to amend that recipe, as no one cooks over a fire anymore. There are other states of animation, however, that don't quite fit into the categories of "alive" or "dead." A few examples follow:

- *A deceased, concurrent, or future part of a living person.* You can connect a deceased, concurrent, or future aspect of a living person, including yourself. How might these tête-à-têtês be beneficial? Imagine that you're talking with a part of your child that lived in a different lifetime. Perhaps that aspect of your living child wants you to remember a special past life gift, such as dancing. This information might compel you to sign her up for dancing lessons in this lifetime.

- *Incoming and outgoing souls.* Souls preparing to enter a physical body frequently want to communicate. They aren't technically dead or alive, as they are leaving the "other side" while taking on the energies of life. An example is a soul visiting with a future mother. As well, exiting (just deceased) souls, frequently called "ghosts," tend to hover on the earth plane for a while. They are neither here nor there and can be seen as sort of living and deceased.

- **Transitional souls.** Some human souls, alive or dead, have previously been an otherworldly being, such as an angel. These "mutant" souls often offer a depth of wisdom and experience.

PAST/PRESENT/FUTURE: As already mentioned several times in this book, you can connect with a being from the past, concurrent present reality, or future. How do you know what you're dealing with? A being speaking in an archaic Scottish accent is probably from ancient Scotland, but if you're not sure, ask! You can also use the tools outlined in the next section.

Analyzing the Sounds and Voices

The actual qualities of a sound or voice can clue you in to the type of source you're dealing with and what its message means. For instance, if a psychic voice is high-pitched, shrill, and demanding—and furthermore turns your stomach—you might think twice about following that source's advice.

Following are sound factors that can help you qualify a source and its validity.

SUBJECTIVE/OBJECTIVE: In order to understand a source's message, you have to figure out if it's providing subjective or objective information. In other words, is a source giving you its opinion or relaying a fact? The following example will explain these points of view.

Imagine that your deceased grandmother has shown up in your bedroom. She says, "I'm concerned about your professional life." Her comment is obviously subjective, as you know that she wouldn't approve of your decision to make your living as an artist. You understand her concern but probably won't change your behavior. Then she says, "You need to sell more paintings to make your car payment." This is an objective (factual) comment, and it might prompt you to get a part-time job until your paintings sell.

Subjective messages aren't better or worse than objective or vice versa. The distinction is important, though. You don't want to interpret a subjective statement as an absolute, and neither do you want to discount an objective fact.

CLOSE/FAR: The location of a voice or sound relative to you can be very revealing. Closer sounds or voices tend to be more intimate. They can also command immediate attention, making you pay attention to the message. If the nearby message is predictive, it's apt to occur soon. Sounds that are farther away are less immediate and more objective; if predictive, they can hint at a further-away event.

HIGH/LOW PITCH: *Pitch* is the term used to distinguish low sounds from high sounds. Usually, higher-pitched sounds are considered more feminine and lower-pitched sounds denote the masculine. Higher pitches can frighten or startle us, and lower pitches might evoke reassurance and stability. As implied, the pitch of a source's voice provides keen insight into the source and its message. For instance, if a highly pitched voice screams "Run!" in your ear, you'll probably run.

TIMING: Timing, or cadence, shapes our interpretation of a message. Consider a voice that pauses frequently. You'll probably believe that the source is wise—or confused, depending on other factors. Based on cadence, you can sometimes determine ethnicity, cultural background, and even the time period from which a voice speaks.

LOUDNESS: Loudness, or the volume of a sound, can
affect our interpretation of a voice. If a source
is really loud, its message will stand out. We'll
feel like saluting. Lower amplitudes, such as
leaves rustling or soft singing, seem more loving,
however. Middle amplitudes usually convey a
communication pertaining to our everyday life.

TONE QUALITY: Is a voice breathy, creaky, or muffled? The amount of air in a voice can indicate
a source's feelings or state of mind. For instance,
if a source speaks in a rushed and breathy voice,
you'll feel like responding quickly. If a source's
voice is low and muffled, you might think it's
hiding something and pry for more information.

What else do you need to know to best analyze a
source and its message? As with sounds, messages can be
categorized. I'll next share these basic categories.

Types of Messages

There are several types of messages that can be delivered
by a source. Figuring out which one a source is presenting
will clue you in on how to respond.

Historical

Historical messages bring up the past or reveal relevant information about you or someone else. We often rely on historical information to figure out the cause of a problem or gain insight into a topic.

Illumination

Some messages illuminate what's really going on. For instance, you might believe that a man you're dating is unmarried. A source might whisper the word "married" in your mind. You perform a search—and break up.

Advice

If you need to make a decision, a source can be sent from the Spirit to offer insight and advice. Still, use your common sense. If a messenger tells you to buy a new house, first check your credit score. You might need to improve it before moving ahead with a house purchase.

Education

Sources often show up to educate or teach. For instance, Christ spoke to me years ago to teach me the Spirit-to-Spirit technique. You might even be lucky enough to get a source to help you with an exam.

The Future

Sources can potentially help us create an optimum future or avoid a negative one. They can also advise you on which steps to take and when to take them. For instance, a couple of years ago the Spirit's voice told me to write a fiction series by a specific date. I obeyed and now am editing the project as I await my next marching order.

● ● ●

All of the above points also can help you interpret environmental sounds.

Environmental Sounds

LISTENING TO THE WORLD

Environmental sounds can hold psychic messages that provide you insights, warnings, messages, and clues. Nearly all of the pointers provided in this chapter for analyzing sources can be applied to environmental noises as well.

For instance, imagine that you're wondering if an illness relates to a situation that occurred in a past life. You hear a *bam* from the other room and rush to see what caused the noise. A book about ancient Greece has fallen on the carpet. You can probably assume that a source pushed the book off the shelf, and you might want to check out what happened to you long ago in Greece.

Frequently sources uses environmental sounds to grab your attention or make a point. Often they do this before or after they communicate more directly. For instance, my radio once turned itself on. The lyrics were about "listening to your angel." That night an angel appeared in my dream and gave me a message about a loved one. I made sure my relative went to the doctor the next day. If I hadn't, they could have suffered a heart attack.

Other times, environmental sounds package a message to underscore one already received. Several years ago I dreamed about my son becoming a major league baseball player. The next day he asked if I would support him in getting the training needed to become...drum roll...a major league baseball player. For the entire next week, every time I overheard a conversation or turned on the television or radio, someone was talking about baseball. Point made and taken.

Know that you can always interpret an environmental sound in the same way you do any other message. Simply conduct Spirit-to-Spirit and ask for a Spirit-appointed source to reveal the message—if there is one—that came in through "surround sound."

CHAPTER 3

There is one more set of qualifiers to pay attention to when channeling. These involve your feelings and bodily senses.

The Role of Feelings and the Bodily Senses

Your feelings and bodily senses are a vanguard for assessing a source and its message. They can help you evaluate a source's intention and the meaning and validity of a message. This section will give you a brief overview of how to interpret your feeling-based and bodily reactions to a source.

The caveat is that many of us were taught to disregard or question our feelings. Anger is bad. Fear opposes love. The truth is that pure feelings, those consisting of the five major feeling constellations, clue us in to our most genuine reactions to a source. These five feeling groups are joy, fear, anger, sadness, and disgust. Each provides us a different understanding about a source and its message.

Many of us have also been taught to ignore our bodies. I was taught to shove through pain and resistance, often to my own disadvantage. However, our senses can key us in to how our deeper self is responding to a source and its message.

Following are ways to interpret what your feelings and bodily sensations might be telling you about a source or its message.

The Five Feeling Constellations

The five main feelings and their meanings are as follows:

JOY: Also felt as peace, calm, happiness, serenity, appreciation, and other positive reactions, this feeling indicates that a source is trustworthy and its advice will better your life.

FEAR: Something is dangerous. This source is telling you to change paths or figure out what is threatening. If you're scared of a source, however, you must question whether or not it is Spirit-approved.

ANGER: A boundary is being violated and must be upheld or set. Figure out if the source is violating your boundary or if it's trying to make you pay attention to a boundary violation.

SADNESS: This source is pointing out an area in which you perceive a lack of love. You need to focus on what will create more love in your life.

DISGUST: The source is either bad for you or showing you something that is bad for you.

Meaning of a Sensory Sensation

The underlying meaning of your body's reactions to a source and its message are as follows. This list is based on the basic physical senses minus hearing.

SMELL: Positive and well-intentioned sources will smell pleasing; sour or foul smells can indicate that the source is trying to deceive you.

TOUCH: Sometimes a source can actually touch you or make you feel as if you're being touched. Does the physical sensation associated with a source or its message leave you feeling comforted or threatened? Does a source make your skin crawl or flush with joy? The body can usually sense what the mind cannot.

TASTE: Taste is a very discriminatory sense. If your mouth floods with a sweet taste when a source speaks, you can probably trust the message. If your mouth fills with a sour taste, the source might be bitter and therefore malintentioned.

SIGHT: We'll examine ways to employ your clairvoyance in chapter 6. For now, know that if you actually see a source psychically, you should assess it as you would a person you've just met. If the source looks mean and cruel, request a different source.

* * * *

Ready to pull all the information presented in this chapter together and practice channeling? Let's do it!

Conducting a Classical Clairaudience Session

This exercise can be used to perform any (or all) of the three types of classical clairaudience. The additional tips offered after this exercise will assist you with specific concerns related to channeling.

STEP 1: **Prepare.** If you desire, grab a stone to help you focus (see page 92 for a list). Settle into a comfortable space. Create an intention for this session and state it aloud. Then tone as you were taught to do in the section beginning on page 93 and select a form of channeling for your interaction: full, partial, or receptive. Ask the Spirit to adjust your brain waves and brain state so you can operate as safely and effectively as

possible during your interaction. If you decide
on full or partial channeling, read through the
tips presented after this exercise to better prepare
yourself.

STEP 2: **Conduct Spirit-to-Spirit.** Affirm your
spirit, others' spirits (including your gatekeeper),
and the Spirit. Then ask the Spirit to summon
an entity or group of entities that can enlighten
you on your selected topic.

STEP 3: **Perform an Initial Qualification.** Focus
on the source. What are your initial reactions?
Don't let a source into your body until you've
analyzed your initial responses to the source.
Instead, ask the source to share a message with
you and pay attention to how that message is
relayed.

As soon as you've established a clear verbal
contact, ask the source to name and describe
itself. You can also evaluate the source using
these steps:

- *Spirit–Approved or Not:* Ask your trusted
  gatekeeper or the Spirit if this is a Spirit-
  approved source. If it isn't, break off contact.

You can also make a statement toward the source, such as "If the Spirit doesn't approve your presence, you must leave." Use healing streams to dismiss a non–Spirit-approved source and ask for an acceptable source to replace it.

- *Assess Your Participation:* Ask the Spirit to affirm that you are actually involved in a clairaudient activity instead of a false one, such as a fantasy or repetitive trauma. Trust the affirmative response in your body or the sound you hear. If you have any doubts, ask for healing streams of grace to disconnect you from this process and decide later how to best approach the issue.

- *Weigh In on Attachments:* Check for energetic attachments or wounds to make sure you aren't being manipulated by a source that is negatively bound to you or stirring an already-existing energetic abnormality. Ask the Spirit directly to reveal any attachments or wounds through your clairvoyance, clairempathy, or clairaudience. If a problem exists, ask for healing streams

to free you and all concerned, and then
ask the Spirit if you should continue with
the current source, ask for another one, or
conclude the session.

- If the source passes the above tests, focus
again on its initial message.

STEP 4: **Engage More Fully.** You can now ask the
Spirit to shift your brain state appropriately and
establish your channeling structure, whether it is
full, partial, or receptive. Even if you're involved
in a full channeling at this point, you'll be able
to hear your own voice and feel your own sense
of the situation from outside of your body. Now
ask for communication and messaging from the
source, and evaluate these in the next steps.

STEP 5: **Gauge the Sound/Voice.** Evaluate the
sound or voice for these qualifiers, as applicable:

- internal/external
- own/other
- single/multiple
- human/otherworldly (can also be natural,
whether earthly or off-world; see chapter 7)
- alive/deceased/other
- past/present/future

- subjective/objective
- close/far
- pitch/timing/timbre/tone

STEP 6: **Assess the Message.** Is the message primarily historical, illuminating, advising, educational, or futuristic? Ask additional questions of the source until the message is more complete.

STEP 7: **Notice Any Environmental Sounds.** Note any environmental sounds and see what they might mean to you.

STEP 8: **Use Your Feelings and Body.** Let your feelings and bodily reactions provide you further insights about the source and its message. If at any time you feel unsafe, you can use healing streams of grace and end the session.

STEP 9: **Finish the Conversation.** Ask additional questions until you are finished with the source's message. If you need to, switch brain states for additional insights.

STEP 10: **Conclude.** When you feel finished, request that healing streams soothe and rebalance your system while lovingly detaching you from the source. Then return to your everyday life.

Additional Tips

PROTECTING YOURSELF DURING FULL TRANSMEDIUMSHIP

There are several ways to better protect yourself when performing full transmediumship. These are the processes that I use.

SET PARAMETERS: Before deliberately conducting a full transmediumship interaction, create and then write down or say aloud your rules. Your guidelines might include the following:

- The entering entity must adjust to my body chemistry rather than the other way around.

- My exiting soul can decide to re-enter at any time and the entering soul must then vacate.

- My gatekeeper can make the above decision for me at any time.

- I will only allow an exchange for _____ minutes.

- The incoming soul must have the following qualities: (select qualities such as kindness, enlightenment, respect, etc.).

- My soul will be held within the Spirit's care when I'm outside of my body.

Now ask that the Spirit or your gatekeeper use healing streams to hold all concerned to these rules.

APPOINT A "CHIEFTAIN": If interacting with multiple entities, have the Spirit appoint a single representative of the group. Only this being can enter your body.

CONSULT A SOUL EXPERT: Select a trusted advisor such as a shaman, energy healer, priest, spiritualist, or an intuitive who works with soul issues to create a safety plan for you. They might instruct you on how to set special stones for protection around your bed, teach you how to return your soul to the body if it's flying around, or hang a dream catcher near your bed (a medicine wheel that keeps you safe at night).

SET SLEEP BOUNDARIES: If you are prone to full transmediumship when sleeping, allow your personal spirit or gatekeeper to serve as a protector so that nothing dangerous happens to you.

USE HEALING STREAMS: Before any interaction
or prior to going to sleep, ask the Spirit to
surround the entity entering your body with
healing streams, thus protecting your body from
its energy. Also ask that your own soul, when
exited, be enfolded within these streams so you
remain safe while outside of your system.

These same rules can be applied to partial transmediumship. For instance, you can surround your own and the other soul with healing streams during the clairaudient interaction, thus protecting all concerned.

Additional Tip
CLEARING A BOTHERSOME SOURCE

Sometimes we inadvertently get dialed in to a source that is bothersome, maybe even worrisome. Perhaps an external voice keeps repeating a sound or message in our head or that enters through our ears, whether we're conducting a deliberate classical clairaudience session or are running around in everyday life. It's also possible that a source's communication gets stuck in our mind and echoes in our own voice, making us feel like we're stuck in a Memorex experiment. Our own inner mind can keep an external entity's sound on "replay."

It's important to determine if a repetitive or irritating sound or voice is interference or a sign of a chemical or emotional imbalance. This subject was first introduced on page 81's section "Additional Points for Discernment." If you believe that the annoying sounds might indicate an emotional or biochemical disturbance, please see a therapist or another professional. If you're clear that the voice or sound is, in fact, *not* a sign of an inner issue, you can conduct the following steps.

STEP ONE: **Conduct Spirit-to-Spirit.** Ask that the Spirit and only the Spirit serves as your clairaudient informant.

STEP TWO: **Ask for Healing Streams.** Request that the Spirit surround the irritating source with healing streams of grace, forming a transparent bubble that is impenetrable.

STEP THREE: **Assess the Interference.** Ask the Spirit to help you psychically see, sense, or hear the source. You want to know what it is, what it's seeking from you, and what makes you vulnerable to it.

STEP FOUR: **Fill in Your Vulnerability.** Let the
Spirit address your vulnerability. What do you
need to know, do, or realize to stop being
exposed to this interference? Let the Spirit
provide you insights, messages, and visions to
clean your personal issues and to then employ
healing streams to fill in any energetic holes,
leaks, cords, or other frailties in your body, mind,
or soul.

STEP FIVE: **Release the Interference.** The Spirit
will now transport the interfering being to
wherever or whenever it needs to be. Experience this release and feel grateful for the shift.
The Spirit will make sure that the released
source will be cared for and that you remain free.
Now continue your life and enjoy the relative
quiet.

If you desire to use guided writing to conduct a process similar to this one, you can undertake the process on
page 172 for dealing with looping messages.

How to Conduct a Séance

Do you want to experience one of the most famous methods of classical clairaudience? The purpose of the traditional séance is to connect with the deceased, although you can employ the same process to receive guidance from a spiritual master, saint, avatar, or even an aspect of a living person.

These steps will enable you to perform a séance using receptive channeling, during which time the medium will communicate with an external soul or group of souls. Even if you are a full or partial medium, you can use the steps provided.

I have described the following steps in third person so that you can either use this process as the medium or as an organizer-participant. The steps involved follow.

STEP 1: **Preplan.** A séance takes preplanning. Figure out these issues:

- *Date, Place, Topic, Entity, People.* Set a date and time; nighttime is best because of its ambiance. Then select a space that has a table, chairs, and adjustable lighting. Select a topic and, if applicable, which entity or type of entity should be invited to speak. The Spirit can also select the entity during the séance. Then create an invitation list—of living people, that is.

- *Prepare the Room.* Make sure that there are enough chairs and dim the lights. You might want to light a candle, set out a stone or a group of stones, and wear comfortable and loose clothing. Séances sometimes employ Ouija boards or tarot cards. This version doesn't use props. If you want to create an audio or audiovisual recording of the event, set up the technology. I've known people who have actually heard spirits rustling or speaking on these audio devices, even though they weren't audible during the event. See if that happens to you!

STEP 2: **Get Started.** The séance is on! Before
beginning, ask all participants to sit and hold
hands. This circle includes the medium. Have
the medium state the purpose of the séance
and then lead the group in a chant. You can use
the fifth chakra seed syllable, which sounds like
"hum," or conduct Spirit-to-Spirit together,
repeating a prayer of protection like the
following:

> *We affirm our personal spirits;*
> *We affirm each other's spirits;*
> *We affirm the Greater Spirit;*
> *We acknowledge that the Greater Spirit*
> *is opening and managing our connection.*

STEP 3: **Open to the Entity or Entities.** The
medium will now open to the source sent by
the Spirit. They can use the process described in
exercise 6 to qualify the source (see page 127).
The medium should also share the received
information aloud, stating the name of the
source and their intentions, as well as any information provided. At some point, the medium
can ask the group members to ask questions
of the invisible source. The types of questions
depend on the issue covered.

If there are environmental sounds, such as whistles or bangs, the medium should ask the source to interpret them.

STEP 4: **Conclude.** When the medium feels like the communication is complete, they should have everyone in the group individually thank the source for showing up. Close the circle by having all participants chant or hum. You can use the fifth chakra syllable, pronounced "hum," or the fourth chakra syllable, "yum." The medium can now request healing streams for all involved, including the source, and then have everyone take a few deep breaths before it's time to release hands. The medium should now initiate a group discussion to share individual perceptions about the experience.

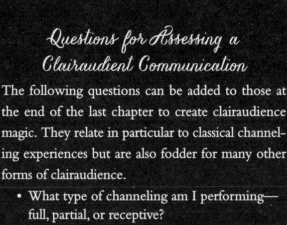

Questions for Assessing a Clairaudient Communication

The following questions can be added to those at the end of the last chapter to create clairaudience magic. They relate in particular to classical channeling experiences but are also fodder for many other forms of clairaudience.

- What type of channeling am I performing—full, partial, or receptive?

- What brain state am I in?

- Should I switch to a different brain state or type of classical channeling?

- What form is the message coming as? (vocalizations, words, noises, music, etc.)

- Is this source Spirit-approved or not? If not, what do I do?

- Am I being influenced by any attachments or wounds? If these exist, shall I use healing streams?

- What is the name of the source?

- What do these sounding factors tell me about the source?
    - internal/external sound/voice
    - own/other voice
    - single/multiple sources
    - alive/deceased/worldly/otherworldly/other
    - past/present/future in origin
- What do these qualities of the sound or voice tell me about the source or the message?
    - subjective/objective
    - close/far
    - pitch/timing/timbre/tone
- What type of message is this:
    - historical?
    - illuminating?
    - advising?
    - educational?
    - futuristic?
- What do any environmental sounds tell me about a source or message?
- What do my feelings and bodily sensations tell me about the source or its message?
- What is the source's overarching message?
- Where do I go from here?

· · · · · ·
Summary

There are three forms of classical clairaudience: full, partial, and receptive. This chapter was chock-full of ways to analyze and interact with a source. You learned how to assess states of awareness and check and interpret a clairaudient message, as well as how to conduct a séance. The information in this chapter will assist you with many of the practices found in the following chapters.

CHAPTER FOUR

Speaking in Tongues

The phrase "speaking in tongues" sounds mysterious, doesn't it? An esoteric ability, speaking in tongues is most frequently examined through a Christian lens, which defines it as the channeling of the Holy Spirit. The truth is that hundreds of cultures employ tongue speaking, or the channeling of divine and foreign languages. After all, everyone is related to the Spirit, and the Spirit can relate to anyone.

In this chapter I'll briefly explore both types of tongue speaking: divine speaking and language speaking. I'll provide examples of both styles and present exercises for awakening and practicing this clairaudient gift. Who knew this amazing capability lies inside each of us?

Two Versions of the Same Channeling Gift

Technically, speaking in tongues is a form of channeling, although it differs from classical channeling in that you are much less interactive with the source. You might not even understand the source. For example, when divine speaking, you basically serve as a channel for the highest forms of spiritual beings, even the Spirit itself. Neither the Spirit nor angels need to speak in English. When language speaking, you either speak in a foreign language or with a foreign accent. In the former case, you'll probably not understand a word. Both forms of tongue speaking, however, can leave you changed and enriched.

After describing the two types of tongue speaking, I'll present an exercise for each. Both exercises will help you "untie your tongue," or loosen the strictures of language, so you can serve as a speaker for unknown languages. Fundamentally, speaking in tongues invites new and inspiring energies into your life.

Divine Speaking

Technically, divine speaking is called *glossolalia*. Glossolalia involves emitting "ecstatic utterances" that contain a supernatural message. Usually the medium is in a blissful state and the communications are believed to come from the Spirit, angels, or other advanced spirits.

Most of the time, the speaker and any listeners don't understand the spirit-based messages. In other words, the words, tones, chants, or songs are often considered gibberish, albeit celestial gibberish.

As pointed out, most Westerners link divine speaking to Christianity ever since the Holy Spirit fell upon Jesus's followers during Pentecost. The believers were then "filled by the Holy Spirit" and began to speak in tongues as the Spirit enabled them (Acts 2:4). Churches around the world have continued teaching and inviting tongue speaking, specifically the divine-speaking variety, mainly because tongue speaking is considered a way to let God speak through you. And even though most divine speakers don't understand the channeled expressions, the Bible suggests it would be good to do so. As stated in 1 Corinthians, tongue speakers should share "one at a time, and someone must interpret," otherwise the speaker should keep the communication between themselves and God (1 Corinthians 14: 27-28). The latter point suggests that although modern tongue speakers might not comprehend the message, it's possible to do so.

Divine speaking is not only a Christian feat, however. It's practiced amongst shamans in Sudan, the Shango in West Africa, the Zor in Ethiopia, the Voodoo in Haiti, and the Aboriginals of South America and Australia, among other cultures and countries (gotquestions.org, "What Is Glossolalia?"). I've heard tongue speakers in Peru, Costa Rica, Morocco, Venezuela, Mexico, and other places. In exercise 8 I'll outline several stepping-stones you can walk upon to bring through and maybe even understand a divine language.

Language Speaking

Every so often, a news article spotlights someone who suddenly started speaking in a foreign language or with a foreign accent. Medically, the phenomenon is called the "Foreign Language Syndrome," and it usually appears in individuals who have suffered a traumatic brain injury or awakened from a coma or have gone through some other unusual precursor, such as a near-death experience. Examples include a Malaysian student who awoke after an accident speaking four new languages, and a young Croatian girl speaking German after being roused from a coma. Although German was her second language, upon awakening she lost her ability to speak Croatian.

Experts believe that the source of Foreign Language Syndrome is damage to the left side of the brain, in particular to the language areas. However, other experts assert that when the symptoms involve only a change in accents and there isn't a brain injury, the cause is genetic mutation (Callaway 2009).

We don't need to be hit on the head or undergo a trauma to potentially perform language speaking, which is technically called *xenoglossy*. Our clairaudience can serve as a tool for speaking in another language or an unusual accent. I know an intuitive who speaks either in a British accent or Sanskrit when working. Her clients can understand the British accent but not the Sanskrit, which she can only comprehend if she performs receptive channeling and asks a guide to interpret the message. A student of mine dreams in the language of the star Antares (a star in the Orion constellation), which she understands implicitly. Both women believe that they used to speak in these languages in previous lives.

Why can we access a foreign language or accent? We might have spoken the articulated language in an earlier lifetime. We might already be conversing in a different language or with an accent in a parallel life. Then again, we might be connecting into a language template through the backside of our fifth chakra, which adjusts our vocal configurations.

Another option is that we're employing our epigenetics. Epigenes are the chemical soup that surround our genes and hold our ancestors' memories, disease patterns, and reactions to events. It's possible that subtle or traumatic energies can activate an ancestor's language and *voilà*, we can access it.

As well, we might connect with an entity from another culture and duplicate their language or accent. This process can involve full, partial, or receptive channeling. For example, I have a client who is instructed by an invisible guide that speaks Chinese. Although my client doesn't understand Chinese, she can mimic the guide's words. She has to have a Chinese-speaking friend interpret the words for her, however.

Why should we try to speak in tongues? Words are symbols that come alive when vocalized. Every language expresses through a unique cadence and rhythm that conveys mental meaning but also delivers subtle energies. You might hear the word "mountain" in German and feel bigger and more powerful. Listen to the word in Greek and you'll want to climb the mountain. The energetics of different languages affect us differently and attune us to various aspects of our personality.

Want to practice both types of speaking in tongues? It's time to play.

Exercise
--8--

Speaking a Divine Language

When performing glossolalia, or divine speaking, we receive a message from the Spirit, an angel, or another highly conscious being. These beings speak in what I call the "language of love" or the "language of light," whether the utterances consist of prose, poetry, song, or some other sound. We can sometimes translate a divine message into our own language so we can understand it. I'll share both steps in this exercise.

STEP 1: **Prepare.** Decide if you want to divine speak by yourself or direct the channeling to another person. It can be easier to have a friend present as this person can remember what you share. With someone or alone, settle into a quiet place and make sure you won't be disturbed.

STEP 2: **Perform Spirit-to-Spirit.** Acknowledge your personal spirit, the helping spirits, and the Spirit. Let the Spirit fill you with angelic love and serenity. Loosen your body, close your eyes, and imagine pictures of light, angels, or other beings of love. Let the Spirit shift you into the appropriate trance or brain state.

STEP 3: **Open Your Mouth.** The key to speaking in tongues is to open your mouth and start making sounds and noises. Babble. Gurgle. Hum. Simultaneously, imagine that the Spirit or a being of light stands behind you and sends sounds from the language of love and light through the backside of your fifth chakra, which is at the rear of your neck. Keep verbalizing while strands of paradise strum through you. Relax into the process and continue to vocalize.

STEP 4: **Look for Repetition.** After several minutes you will notice repetitive sounds. As soon as this occurs, know that you are divine speaking.

STEP 5: **Give In to the Flow.** Fall further into a
trance state and feel the streams of energy pouring through every part of you. As you continue
vocalizing, sense the energies in your bones. If
you feel like moving, do so. Bask in this current
of love as long as you desire. If you feel like it's
enough to simply channel this language without
comprehending it, move to step 7 when ready.
Otherwise, perform the next step.

STEP 6: **Translate in Your Natural Language.**
Still uttering the divine sounds, ask that the
Spirit transcribe the spiritual language into your
natural language. You'll sense the Spirit interacting through the backside of your fifth chakra or
in your brain to perform the translation. Simply continue speaking until the words become
recognizable.

STEP 7: **Close.** Your vocalizing will wind down
organically. Spend a few minutes in the ensuing
stillness, confer with a companion if you have
one, and then return to your everyday reality.

Exercise
-9-

Clairaudient Language Speaking

As shared earlier in this chapter, there are two main ways to experience language speaking. One is to stimulate the shift inside of yourself. Quite specifically, you can awaken the language part of your brain, receive spiritual energy through your fifth chakra, open to a language from a past life self, or bring through a language coded into your epigenetic material. The second major way to access a different language is to channel an external entity.

This exercise will guide you through all the just-shared processes. I'll help you understand what you are speaking if you conduct this exercise alone. It can be easier, however, to have a person assist you. When speaking in tongues, we have to strike a balance between letting go and being aware. If you want, select a person to guide you through these steps and instruct you on the way.

STEP 1: **Prepare.** Find a quiet space and make sure you won't be disturbed. If you are with a trusted partner, ask that they too be silent. If you want, give

them the job of reading these steps aloud so you
can follow them. Now allow the Spirit to shift you
into the most beneficial trance or brain state.

STEP 2: **Conduct Spirit-to-Spirit.** Acknowledge
your own spirit, that of the helping spirits, and
the Spirit.

STEP 3: **Internally Open to a Different Language.** Ask the Spirit to activate your internal
ability to speak in a different language or foreign
accent in whatever way is correct for you. You
might feel a part of your brain awaken, sense
a flow of spiritual energy through your backside fifth chakra, feel a past life self activate, or
become aware of the stirring of your epigenetic
or ancestral material. Loosen your mouth and
tongue and begin to hum, chant, or babble. Let
your sounds free-flow until you sense that a language or accent is emerging. Don't fixate on the
language; simply utter the sounds.

Continue with this outpouring and then ask
the Spirit to change the language or accent into
your own language so that you can hear the
meaning of the message just shared. This alteration might occur slowly or quickly. Just keep
speaking until the transference has completed

and you run out of words. (Your assistant can also write down the translation of what you are speaking.)

When silent, ask the Spirit or your gatekeeper if there is a reason that you were able to access that specific language or accent. Have you ever spoken it before? Has an ancestor? Did that language alter you in some sort of beautiful and subtle way? What ultimate message are you to glean from this process? Let these answers come through your clairaudience from the Spirit or your gatekeeper and then either move on to step 4 or 5 when ready.

STEP 4: **Connect with a Foreign Entity.** Take a few deep breaths and allow the Spirit to link you with a foreign-speaking entity. Qualify this source using the tips you've learned in the last three chapters. Then employ full, partial, or receptive channeling to hear the being speak within your mind. See if you can understand what is being shared, then open your mouth and ask the Spirit to establish you as a conduit for the message. You will literally speak in the language or with the accent of the source.

Now ask the Spirit to shift the foreign language into one that you can recognize. Ask that the source repeat itself or add new information to this understandable tongue speaking until you run out of words. Then spend a few moments in reflection.

STEP 5: **Close.** Ask that healing streams disconnect you from all entities and energies used in this exercise, and rebalance your personal energy. Ponder what you've learned for a few minutes before returning to your life.

Additional Tip

SOUNDING YOURSELF OPEN

Return to chapter 2's section "Tones for Attunement" on page 93. Before beginning either exercise, chant the fifth chakra seed syllable and then run through each of the chakra sounds from one to seven. Return to the fifth chakra seed syllable and vocalize it for as long as you want. Sing these "scales" over and over to loosen up your throat for tongue speaking.

Questions for Assessing a Clairaudient Communication

These questions can help you with speaking in tongues.

- Is it appropriate for me to speak in tongues?

- If it is, should I open to the following:

  - divine speaking?
  - language speaking?
    - *from inside myself; if so, through what means?*
  - brain part?
  - fifth chakra stimulation?
  - past life self?
  - epigenetic material?
    - *by channeling an entity*

- How can I best understand tongue speaking?

- After performing a tongue speaking, what is my takeaway?

* * * * * * *

Summary

Speaking in tongues involves bringing through an unknown language. There are two styles that employ this clairaudient channeling process. Glossolalia, or divine speaking, relies on channeling a spiritual language. Most typically the syllables or sounds uttered aren't understandable, but some people are able to interpret the messages. Xenoglossy, or language speaking, invites communicating in a foreign language or with a foreign accent. You learned how to perform both styles in this chapter.

CHAPTER FIVE

* * * *

Clairaudient Writing

One of my favorite forms of clairaudience is clairaudient writing. As a child I wrote plays, stories, and fables. Looking back, I believe that I was frequently accessing my clairaudience when writing. Guess what? I'm still using this ability for a variety of writing purposes.

There are two main types of clairaudient writing: guided and automatic. Through this chapter you'll learn the basics of each style and participate in an exercise designed to help you explore both forms of writing. I'll also show you how to send healing energy through clairaudient writing, a holy endeavor if there is one. No matter what unfolds through your pen, pencil, or computer, it will be a discourse of great interest and beauty.

What Is Clairaudient Writing?

Clairaudient writing is a form of channeling conducted with writing. All clairaudient capabilities work through the fifth chakra. Because it's performed through the hands and arms, which are extensions of the heart area, clairaudient writing also employs the fourth chakra.

As with all mediumship activities, clairaudient writing invites connection to multiple sources. You can bring through or call upon parts of yourself, living or deceased persons, and otherworldly beings. As with all major forms of channeling, you'll want to use the sourcing qualifiers and safety mechanisms you've been acquiring in earlier chapters.

I believe that clairaudient writing is much more popular and widespread than anyone knows. In chapter 1 I showcased a few of the famous greats who knowingly accessed their clairaudience to bring forth music and literature. I can't help but wonder how many people perform channeled writing without realizing it.

Think of how often you've been caught up in something you're writing. Maybe the masterpiece was a haiku, sonnet, set of lyrics, musical composition, jingle, quip, press release, marketing brochure, essay, story, article, memo, thesis outline, or even a chapter for a book. When the concept or flow comes effortlessly, you might be employing channeled writing.

As I said, there are two basic types of clairaudient writing. Guided writing utilizes partial or receptive channeling. Basically, the words or expressions come from a source greater than your everyday self. Your soul remains in your body while you're writing, although another being can also share your body during the process.

Automatic writing relies on partial or full channeling. This means that you are co-authoring with an internalized being or you've stepped out for a spell while a source writes through your body.

When you are performing partial channeling, which involves a connection to another soul, it can be helpful to figure out how deeply you are letting the external soul in or not; in other words, how much full versus partial channeling is involved in a clairaudient interaction. That insight will clue you in to how much of the clairaudient data comes from your soul versus the other's soul. The answer is that you gauge based on a continuum. In general, the less of you involved or present in clairaudient writing, the more "full" the mediumship involved. If you are able to still edit or alter a writing, your partial channeling is more oriented toward receptive. In the end, it might not even matter, as long as you feel safe and fulfilled.

Now let's look at each version of clairaudient writing and a few examples of each.

Guided Writing
A Matter of Opening to Flow

Plain and simple, guided writing allows you to receive and write when your soul is in your body, although you can also invite another entity or group of entities to share your body and their wisdom. I know I'm participating in guided rather than everyday writing when I'm aware of a source of energy or information that feels bigger than my everyday self. My written words seem "more than normal." Typically, I also experience an uncanny ability to understand the material, flow with the process, and remain focused on the project goals.

There are near-limitless guided writing sources, including aspects of myself as well as external beings. For instance, I'm writing a science fiction series featuring a self I was in a past life on another planet. I also engage with numerous external resources to help me research nonfiction writing projects.

In general, my guided writing expeditions involve two steps. Firstly, I receive a download and the words pour through me. Then I connect to "editing guides," beings that help me select specific words and punctuate correctly. Sometimes I come up with such unusual phrases that I wonder about the source, only to discover that the guidance lived a few hundred years ago.

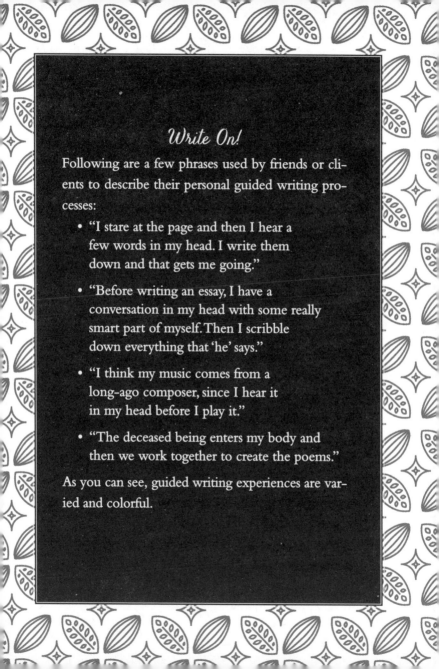

Write On!

Following are a few phrases used by friends or clients to describe their personal guided writing processes:

- "I stare at the page and then I hear a few words in my head. I write them down and that gets me going."

- "Before writing an essay, I have a conversation in my head with some really smart part of myself. Then I scribble down everything that 'he' says."

- "I think my music comes from a long-ago composer, since I hear it in my head before I play it."

- "The deceased being enters my body and then we work together to create the poems."

As you can see, guided writing experiences are varied and colorful.

Automatic Writing

GOING WITH THE FLOW OF WISDOM

As occurs with all channeled writing, automatic writing relies on the fourth and fifth chakras, though in particular it employs partial or full mediumship.

Overall, automatic writing has a supernatural quality to it. My personal experience is fairly predictable. I stare at paper or a computer screen, trying to be brilliant, and my brain goes on vacation. Sometime later, I look down and am shocked to read words that don't sound like my own.

People can use automatic writing to create anything from scientific formulas to business proposals. I have a friend who employs guided writing to author books featuring the channelings of deceased American presidents.

Do you know if you've experienced automatic writing? Maybe you do, maybe you don't. We don't often talk about this ability in our sanitized culture. Recently, however, I read about an author who wrote a book in a week. He barely slept or ate and didn't know what he had written until the book was finished. The product needed very little editing. I have a sense that he was conducting automatic writing.

Others I know have described their interactions with automatic writing in these ways:

- "A being I called 'the Presence' enters me and I blank out. The words he leaves on my paper are more beautiful than any an angel could compose."

- "Every so often I'm filled with a 'have to.' I *have to* write. I'm in my body, but it's like my smart self is in there too. It's how I write my research papers."

- "When I don't have a clue about a concern, I 'set myself aside' and ask God to send me a helper. Suddenly the wisdom is inscribed on the paper."

Because automatic writing requires a loss of control, it's important to be safe when performing it. My recommendation is to choose your timetable and put the Spirit in charge of all automatic writing sessions.

What do I mean by "choose your timetable"? I once worked with a client who was awakened every night to channel written messages from beings in the Orion constellation. The group would occupy her body while she "tuned out." When the star beings exited and she had returned, she'd feel shaky and nauseous. The visiting souls resonated at such a different frequency that her body reacted violently to their presence. The writings they left echoed with sentiment and beauty, but she questioned whether the process was worth it.

I advised my client to establish a set time for the automatic writing during the day and only allow a single Orion representative into her body. She even set the kitchen timer so they had to exit after twenty minutes. I also asked her to put the Spirit in charge of all interactions so that if anything went awry, the automatic writing session would be immediately ended.

My client's health improved dramatically and she started to really enjoy her channeling experiences. If these measures hadn't sufficed, I would have recommended that she shift from automatic to guided writing.

Exercise
--10--

Writing Through Clairaudience

This exercise will help you perform clairaudient writing through guided writing, automatic writing, or both.

STEP 1: **Prepare.** Sit at a table or desk with your writing instruments. You can lower the lights but make sure that you can see well enough to write. If you desire, play music or hum the syllables associated with the fourth and fifth chakras, which sound like "yum" and "hum," respectively. Formulate a specific question, desire, or task, and write it down. Then spend a few minutes breathing until you're in a light trance, perhaps in beta, theta, or another of the brain states explained in chapter 3.

STEP 2: **Conduct Spirit-to-Spirit.** Affirm your personal spirit, the helping spirits, and the Spirit. Spend a few minutes drifting deeper into your trance state—but don't nod off! Ask that your energetic anatomy, specifically your fourth and fifth chakras, be safely opened for your writing experience.

STEP 3: **Request Assistance.** Ask the Spirit or your gatekeeper to connect you with the most appropriate provider of assistance while keeping your soul in your body.

STEP 4: **Sense the Source.** Is it a part of you?
Another being? Is a group involved? Qualify the
source using the questions posed at the end of
the last few chapters, checking for the source's
nature, style of communicating, and all other
pertinent factors. Muse upon the responses
you've been given or write them down.

Remain connected to the source while you
ask the Spirit if you should next perform step 5
or skip to step 6. You can also first conduct step
5 and then step 6.

STEP 5: **Perform Guided Writing.** Ask the source
to connect with you via guided writing. It will
either remain outside of you or enter your body,
although you'll remain firmly anchored inside as
well. Flex your fingers and then take a few deep
breaths and begin writing. You'll sense that your
arms and hands are extensions of your heart and
you are being guided to write what you hear or
simply flows through you.

Keep writing until you feel complete and
then check in with the Spirit or your gatekeeper.
Should you next perform automatic writing or
jump to the closing step?

STEP 6: **Perform Automatic Writing.** Establish parameters for an automatic writing process, including establishing a timetable and putting the Spirit or your gatekeeper in charge of the process. Now take a few deep breaths and sit in silence for a few minutes. Ask the Spirit to shift you into the appropriate brain state; I recommend gamma. In gamma you will be fully physically aware and yet completely open to spiritual messages.

When you feel calm about the task ahead, ask the Spirit or your gatekeeper to invite the source into your body. Healing streams of grace will surround the source and also your own soul, which is now held in love outside your body. The source will now write, and the Spirit will end the session at the appropriate time.

STEP 7: **Close.** Take a few deep breaths and use healing streams to disconnect from any sources and integrate back into your life. Read what you have written and then thank the Spirit for the help, returning to your daily life when ready.

Additional Tip

DEALING WITH LOOPING MESSAGES

Sometimes a being creates more frustration than clarity when we're performing automatic or guided writing. The message might loop around, never really answering a question or creating clarity. We might even feel like the messenger is playing with us, leading us to believe that it has no intention of making sense—or ever letting us go.

When we're performing automatic writing, we're not going to observe either of these phenomena until we're done writing and reading what has been written. If we've been exercising guided writing, we might become confused while we're writing; certainly, we'll sense confusion when we're finished with a session. No matter the case, we must make sure that we're only working with—and opening to—Spirit-approved sources, and that if we've been comprised by an interfering source, we can free ourselves from it.

As a guideline, anytime you become muddled during a partial or receptive clairaudient writing session or experience, simply stop. Perform Spirit-to-Spirit and exit the session, and then take the steps I'm going to suggest here. If you have concerns after an automatic writing event, or even after a full-on channeling experience, you can also perform the next steps, which involve figuring out and clearing the reasons that you are vulnerable to possible manipulation.

The truth is that sources can only mess with us if we're open to their influence at some level. This means that we need to address the reason that we're vulnerable and close that loophole. Of course, it's possible that we're also resisting the insights from a source because we don't really want to receive the information. Either way, we must clean ourselves in order to become clearer.

The following process will assist you with this issue. Before conducting it, grab a pen and paper. You'll be using guided writing to gain needed insights.

Perform Spirit-to-Spirit. State aloud that you will only allow the Spirit to work with you. Now ask the Spirit to help you write down a response to this question:

Was the source actually Spirit-approved?

If you wrote down a yes, proceed down track 1 and respond to those questions. If the response was a no, move to track 2.

TRACK 1/YES: Ask these questions of the Spirit:

1. Why did you (the Spirit) allow the confusing source to interface with me?

2. What am I supposed to learn?

3. Is there an aspect of me that needs healing?

4. How can I shift internally so that I don't channel this or another interfering source again?

Listen to the advice given and make any changes indicated. Then thank the Spirit and go about your day.

TRACK 2/NO: Request that the Spirit provide information in response to these questions:

1. What vulnerability within me allowed contact with a non-approved source?

2. What situation or belief system created this soft spot?

3. What do I need to understand or receive in order to eliminate my susceptibility?

4. Will you now help me make the required transformation and protect me from this point on?

Spend a few minutes feeling any shifts in your physical or subtle anatomies, and then return to your normal life.

Know that you can always check and recheck for energetic vulnerabilities. Don't ever feel embarrassed; simply see these types of episodes as useful for pointing out areas to clean and heal.

Additional Tip

SENDING HEALING
THROUGH GUIDED WRITING

I love using guided writing to send healing energy to another person. After asking the subject if they would like you to perform this maneuver, gather your writing instruments. Breathe deeply and write down your healing request or prayer. You'll be using exercise 10 as a base.

Settle into a meditative state and conduct Spirit-to-Spirit. Take a few deep breaths, and ask the Spirit to link you with a healing source. You might specifically request a master, avatar, deceased healer, angel, or other higher form of guidance. Qualify the source, and then request a message for the person in need.

Simply write down whatever comes to you. Don't edit. Write until the message seems complete, then ask the Spirit to separate you from the source, thanking it for its loving assistance. When the message is complete, ask for healing streams to release you and the source and also to rebalance you. Finally, request that the Spirit infuse the written message with healing streams. Words carry power, and when sent to the person in need, the message will have a double effect. When you return to your everyday life, know that in sending the message to the person in need, you'll be delivering a prayer in written form.

Questions for Assessing a Clairaudient Communication

The following questions can be added to those you've been collecting from previous chapters. These relate to clairaudient writing:

- Would it be beneficial to receive help via clairaudient writing?

- Would the subject be best served by performing guided or automatic writing or both?

- Would it be appropriate to send healing to another or others through clairaudient writing?

• • • • • •

Summary

Clairaudient writing involves using the fourth and fifth chakras to bring through written messages while in a trance state. There are two styles of clairaudient writing: guided and automatic. Guided writing employs receptive or partial channeling and assumes you are aware of the writing process. Automatic writing uses partial or full mediumship. Because of this, your level of process awareness might vary. You can use clairaudient writing to bring through anything—from poetry and music to prose and business communications, and also to send healing to others.

CHAPTER SIX

• • • •

Clairaudient Telepathy
CHANGING EMPATHY
INTO TELEPATHY

How many times have you wanted to hear what someone else is thinking? How often have you heard what someone else is thinking? The mental transference of thoughts is one type of telepathy, but there are three other versions of this clairaudient gift.

Quite literally, the word *telepathy* means "distant" (*tele*) and "feeling, perception, passion, affliction, and experience" (*pathos*). Taken as a whole, telepathy is about picking up on all sorts of empathic sensations and transforming them into understandable messages. Clairaudience is exactly the tool needed to turn perceptions into recognizable communications.

Most likely, this broad definition of telepathy is new to you. However, it is the most thorough one. Every chakra houses a gift, and all the chakras communicate with each other. Why wouldn't our clairaudience draw upon the physical knowledge processed by our first chakra or the feelings produced in our second chakra? Why wouldn't we be able to translate the thoughts of another person's third chakra into decipherable words or transmute the spiritual acumen of an angel into a song? All this and more is possible through the process of changing empathically collected information into clairaudient telepathy.

In order to explore all aspects of telepathy and help you experience them, I'll begin this chapter with a brief explanation of empathy and how it works. I'll also offer succinct descriptions of the four main empathic styles we'll be addressing. I'll then present a section on each of the four styles, as well as an exercise devoted to each. By the time you're finished with this chapter, you'll be ready to read minds—or sensations, feelings, and perceptions.

Our Telepathic Connections

Telepathy is the child of a marriage between empathy and clairaudience. As such, it involves the transformation of empathic data into clairaudient sounds. It's key to note that telepathy is rooted in empathy.

What exactly is empathy? Usually empathy is defined as the ability to sense in our bodies what is occurring outside of ourselves. However, it can also involve the ability to read what our own bodies, emotions, and sensitivities are communicating to our greater self. We are all empathic in that we are all biologically hardwired to attune to our own and others' feelings, needs, desires, motivations, and well-being through a complex interaction between our nervous system, hormones, and electromagnetic activity. Not only can we compassionately relate to other living people, but we can also empathize with the dead and all worldly and otherworldly beings. If you are interested in finding out more about this exciting subject, see my book *The Spiritual Power of Empathy.*

From a subtle perspective, I've already discussed one of the ways we receive and disseminate empathic information. Subtle energy enters and exits through individual auric layers before it is transported to a field's corresponding chakra. These chakras then share data amongst themselves and chat with the brain. The intriguing book *Spiritual Telepathy: Ancient Techniques to Access the Wisdom of Your Soul* outlines yet other means of transferring subtle data (Mauro 2015a). By and large, indigenous tribes situate the governance of telepathic communications in the abdominal or solar plexus areas.

In particular, Hawaiian kahuna healers perceive subtle energy threads emanating from the solar plexus/third chakra area. These act like sticky spiderwebs that link one person or being to another. Information passes through the threads like electricity through a wire. The African Bushmen envision similar energy lines that connect people between their belly buttons, while the Australian aboriginals assert that a person's soul, which they locate in the abdominal area, can see and hear from a distance (Mauro 2015b).

I affiliate these parts of the body with the first, second, and third chakras. Respectively, these chakras manage physical, emotional, and mental empathy. This bodily area is also host to the enteric nervous system, a sort of second brain that governs our gastrointestinal tract and also influences mood and emotion. In fact, this second or gut brain employs the same neurotransmitters for regulating thoughts and attitudes as does the brain, hence the probable reason that so many indigenous cultures perceive the abdominal area as being in charge of empathic energies.

To this list of the chakras—one, two, and three—I add another to our catalogue of vital empathic chakras. The seventh chakra, on the top of the head, manages our spiritual connections. It is the home of spiritual empathy, a means for understanding higher spiritual truths and the Spirit's will. Every one of these four empathy-based chakras can be coupled with the fifth chakra to transform empathic sensations into clairaudient activities. Thus does empathy create telepathy in the following four ways:

Primal Instinct (First Chakra)

We can't meet our higher needs, such as the compelling desire for bonding, love, and unity, unless we are safe and secure. Our first chakra is in charge of our survival, constantly alerting us to dangers and opportunities through physical sensations. It's hard to distinguish the meaning of our body's physical messages, however. Is a quickened heartbeat an indicator of a hazardous event or an exciting adventure? By turning a physical sensation into a telepathic or clairaudient message, you can take appropriate action.

Emotional Sensitivities (Second Chakra)

What is a feeling telling you? Is that sudden bolt of anger encouraging you to yell or walk away? Does an overwhelming sadness belong to you or to someone else? We can better differentiate between our own feelings and others' feelings, and gauge the meaning of a personal emotion, when we add a verbal cue. We accomplish this goal by transforming an empathically received emotional message into a telepathic communication.

Mental Knowledge (Third Chakra)

Our third chakra is constantly administering our own and others' thoughts and beliefs through the mental empathy process. By changing the third chakra's data into fifth chakra knowledge, we can better understand (or hear) what we or others are actually thinking.

You can also attune to another's thoughts through a straightforward transference of data between your own and another's fifth chakras. While this activity doesn't technically qualify as empathic, it is telepathic. Because both processes involve the translation of mental data, I'll show you how to accomplish both in this chapter.

Spiritual Awareness (Sixth and Seventh Chakras)

By using our seventh chakra, we become aware of higher spiritual forces through a process called spiritual empathy. A prophetic insight can be nebulous and confusing, as it is sensed as an insubstantial awareness. To help out, our sixth chakra sometimes links with our seventh chakra, adding psychic visions. Whether we are working with a free-standing seventh chakra message or a joint project between the sixth and seventh chakras, transforming the message into a clairaudient reflection can help us make practical decisions that reflect our spiritual desires.

The other strong empathic chakra is the fourth chakra. You'll learn how to hone this chakra's healing powers for clairaudient purposes in chapter 8.

As I more completely examine these four telepathic categories, I'll stop after each explanation to walk you through a customized exercise.

Primal Telepathy
THE ART OF SAFETY

Have you ever been overwhelmed by a physical sensation that alerted you to danger? Maybe you started shaking for no reason, only to discover that something challenging occurred to a loved one at that same moment. Or maybe you felt a thrill and something great happened right afterward. Our bodies are empathic machines, hardwired to life's perils and opportunities. As an example of the latter, I'll share a story about my first and last visit to a casino.

My boyfriend at the time took me to a casino and began betting at the tables while I wandered around. I ambled near a row of slot machines. Next to a specific one, my body lit up. I was nervous; I'd never gambled before. But I was so impassioned that I put in a quarter and won about 125 dollars. I kept the money and haven't gambled since. I figure it was a one-off.

From a chakra point of view, my first chakra had just performed one of its main tasks, which is to provide us with physically empathic messages. It's not always easy to figure out what a body-based signal is suggesting, however. I would have been less nervous if the first chakra data had been accompanied by a telepathic insight, like a loud voice that shouted, "Play this slot machine!"

In general, by transforming a physical knowing into a verbal cue, we can better assure our own and another's fundamental safety, avoid or cope with physical danger and stress, and enhance our financial, sexual, and bodily well-being. The following exercise will teach you how to metamorphose a physically empathic signal into a telepathic or clairaudient message. Know that if you have picked up a sensation from someone else, this will become clear in the process, specifically in step 4.

From Physical Empathy to Physical Telepathy

This exercise can be conducted while you're experiencing a physical sensation that seems meaningful or to check into one previously felt. The physical sensation you're attuning to might belong and pertain to you or to someone or something else.

There is another option: you might be hearing a loud environmental sound, one so startling that your physical body reacts. You'll be shown how to deal with this potentiality in this exercise.

STEP 1: **Be Aware.** Concentrate on the physical sensation you're seeking to understand. If you're responding to a loud environmental sound, one that has shocked your body, focus on your bodily reaction. Without judgment, remain focused on this bodily area. If you desire, grab some paper and a pen. You might want to perform guided writing or take notes.

STEP 2: **Conduct Spirit-to-Spirit.** Affirm your spirit, the helping spirits, and the Spirit.

STEP 3: **Transfer the Sensation.** Still concentrating on the physical sensation, which is the first chakra's purview, ask the Spirit to transfer its energy via healing streams to the center of your fifth chakra.

STEP 4: **Activate and Access Your Clairaudience.** Request that the Spirit send additional healing streams to transform the sensations, held within your fifth chakra, into verbal sounds.

You'll perceive an internal or external translation of the first chakra's message. Listen to this message, speak it aloud, or write it down. Make sure that you evaluate the source of the information as you've been shown to do.

Also make sure to ask if the message relates to you or to someone or something else. If it belongs to someone else, ask the Spirit if or how you should relay the message to them. If the message is pertinent to you, ask questions of the Spirit or the source for advice on how to respond to the message. Continue asking questions until you feel complete.

Step 5: **Close.** Thank the Spirit and your spiritual helpers for their assistance and decide how to follow up on any insights. As you move back into your life, watch for positive changes in your physical demeanor. Repeat this exercise later if you have lingering physical symptoms.

Feeling Telepathy
Hearing the Messages

Feelings are the province of the second chakra, which occupies a significant part of the enteric nervous system territory. It is here that we feel our own and others' feelings.

We've all felt others' feelings with (or for) them. You have dinner with a friend who is crying; pretty soon, you're crying into your own soup. This empathic bond is crucial to compassion, but it can play havoc internally. We can't process feelings that aren't our own. As well, others' feelings, if internalized, can prevent us from owning and responding to our own feelings.

The main purpose of the following exercise is to help you attune empathically to a personal feeling and transform it into a telepathic message. Because it's more critical to relate to your own feelings than process another's, this exercise will separate out others' feelings so you can put words to your own. If at some point it seems fitting to interpret another's feelings telepathically, you can use this same exercise toward that end, just don't release others' emotions in step 4. Instead, transfer the ball of another's feeling-energy into your fifth chakra and transform it into a clairaudient message.

Exercise
–12–

Telepathically Speaking Your Feelings

This exercise will help you shift a personal feeling to your fifth chakra and then spin it into a verbal communication.

STEP 1: **Prepare.** Focus on an emotion that you are currently experiencing or think back to one that requires clarification. Have a pen and paper available if you want to record insights.

STEP 2: **Conduct Spirit-to-Spirit.** Affirm your spirit, others' spirits, and the Spirit. Take a few deep breaths and settle into your body.

STEP 3: **Feel Those Feelings.** While concentrating on your feeling, check for additional emotions. If there aren't any, move to step 5.

If you're aware of multiple emotions, embrace them all. Then ask the Spirit to separate the feelings into two distinct spheres of energy. The first orb will be composed of others' feelings, and the second will be made of your own feelings. If all the feelings are your own, skip to step 5. If not, perform the next step and then continue onward.

STEP 4: **Release Others' Feelings.** Request that the Spirit apply healing streams to release the ball of others' feelings. You might physically feel a relief in your abdomen and a lightening of your load. The Spirit will kindly restore these emotions to their rightful hosts.

STEP 5: **Speak Your Feelings.** Whether you have a single feeling or multiple feelings of your own, ask the Spirit to send the root feeling into your fifth chakra. Healing streams will continue to work on any leftover emotions.

Now request that additional streams flow into the feeling-energy in your fifth chakra and convert it into a telepathic communiqué. You might hear an internal or external vocalization or open your mouth and simply speak aloud. You can also reach for the pen and paper and write down the data flowing through you. If you require additional assistance, ask the Spirit, your gatekeeper, or a divinely approved source for other illuminations. Qualify any unknown source, as you've been taught to do in earlier chapters, before believing its input. Continue this process until you completely understand the message your feeling is trying to share. You can return to the section "The Five Feeling Constellations" on page 125 to review the main theme linked to each emotion.

CLOSE: Thank the Spirit and decide how to honor your feeling's message when you return to your normal life.

Mental Telepathy

WHERE MIND MEETS MATTER

This classic form of telepathy involves hearing another's thoughts in your head. There are actually dozens of different types of telepathic events. The simplest version involves hearing what someone else is thinking while they are thinking it. While acknowledging that it doesn't take a huge psychic ability to know that our child is thinking "no way" after we ask them to clean their room, if a voice in your head or entering through your ears doesn't sound like your own, you are performing mental telepathy.

It's also possible to pick up on what someone said or thought in the past, even if you weren't present at the time. I have an acquaintance whose thoughts give him away every time he's sharing a "tall tale" aloud. One time I was sitting in the bleachers while he told a group of baseball parents that his son had hit a home run for another team the week before. As convoluted as it sounds, I could hear the thoughts he had really thought when his son was playing the previous week: "My son couldn't get a home run for nothing."

Not only had the man's son not earned a home run, but his father's previous thoughts gave him away.

Yet another time, the man bragged about himself, insisting that he had scored the winning touchdown for a playoff game when he was in high school. How did I know that didn't happen? I actually heard his former coach's voice saying, "You cost us that game."

Yet another possibility is that we might hear someone's words or thoughts before they are spoken or thought. Sometimes people think I talk over them because I don't wait for them to finish a sentence. I am a bit overeager. Half the time, however, I hear what the person is going to say before they say it. I once had a male friend state, "Since you know what I'm going to decide, maybe you can tell my conclusions before I make them."

No matter how your mind-to-mind communication shows up, there are two basic ways of performing it.

The first process relies on sharing data between your own and another's fifth chakras. This activity isn't actually empathic in nature. Thoughts really can transfer from one brain to another and be heard through the physical and subtle mechanisms related to the fifth chakra. A little-known fact, however, is that we can also shift subtle energy from our third chakra to our fifth chakra and transform it into verbalizations. The third chakra is empathic in nature; in particular, it picks up on mental data in a process called *claircognizance*, or "clear knowing." I'll show you how to perform both techniques, but first I want to discuss the matter of mind-to-mind communication.

One of the most popular questions about mysticism is whether or not mind-to-mind communication or mental telepathy is real. Many auspicious greats across time have believed that it is, including Dr. Albert Einstein, who regarded telepathy as a matter of physics, not only psychism. Since Einstein's statement, dozens of studies have emphasized the validity of mental telepathy. Others have explained how it might work.

One study in particular involved sending thoughts to sleeping people. The evidence showed that these thoughts influenced the recipients' dreams, as if through "dream telepathy." Yet another study featured the sharing of thoughts and impressions between individuals at a distance. A person would sketch an image and then psychically send the pictures to a recipient, who would draw what they perceived. In these and other studies, the results of the telepathic communication far exceeded random chance (Walia 2015).

Scientists have been seeking to explain mind-to-mind transmission since 2013. The key is knowing that thoughts are composed of electrical and electromagnetic signals. The brain communicates within itself and other parts of the body via these signals but also uses the same process to exchange data with the environment. Proving the point, researchers in one particular study used a combination of monitors to send the encoded frequency of specific words from the brain of a sender located in India to the brain of a recipient in France. The recipient received and correctly interpreted the words (IFL Science, n.d.).

The brain doesn't need technology to encode, send, and decode the thoughts of others. In fact, the brain is able to generate weak electrical fields across levels of neurons (Dockrill 2016), and it can also detect these fields outside of the body (Moisse 2010). And herein we see how subtle energy is transported from person to person or mind to mind. Physical energy is transported on waves of energy, and so is subtle energy.

From a subtle point of view, you merely have to be on the same "brain wave" or "vibe" as a person sending thoughts to pick up on them. This telepathic ability isn't limited to brain-to-brain connections, however. Your third and fifth chakras and their related auric fields also serve as antennae.

Can you learn how to translate another's thoughts into words? I'll show you how to do so. You'll need a partner, though—someone whose thoughts you want to read.

Exercise
--13--

Practicing Mental Telepathy with a Partner

This exercise should be conducted with a partner who has given permission for you to read their mind.

First, you will be interconnecting your third chakra with your partner's third chakra, thus collecting mental data empathically. Then you will transfer this information to your own fifth chakra and put a voice to it. Then you will undertake the next step, which is to link your fifth chakra to their fifth chakra, discovering what additional information makes itself available. It will be interesting for you to compare and contrast these two ways of operating as a mental telepath.

STEP 1: **Prepare.** Double check that your partner is willing to let you read their mind and set aside about a half hour to practice. Ask them to read through this entire exercise so they know what to expect, especially the fact that in step 4 you'll be channeling your perceptions of their thoughts. Then face each other in chairs about three feet apart. Your partner will be the sender, and you will be the recipient.

STEP 2: **Conduct Spirit-to-Spirit.** Both you and your partner should conduct Spirit-to-Spirit together. I recommend that you read the following statement aloud, either one at a time or simultaneously:

> *We affirm our personal spirits,*
> *which are our immortal selves.*
>
> *We acknowledge the other's spirit,*
> *as well as those of our helpers.*
>
> *Together we acknowledge the presence of the Spirit*
> *and surrender this experience to that Spirit.*

STEP 3: **Create a Focus.** Ask your partner (the sender) to silently ruminate on a topic with their eyes closed. Tell them to focus on this topic with all their inner senses: physical, emotional, verbal, and visual. Ask the sender to nod their head when they feel fully caught up in the topic.

STEP 4: **Perform Third Chakra Clairaudience.** Silently request that the Spirit interconnect your third chakra and your partner's third chakra with healing streams. Both of you should close your eyes. Now silently ask that the Spirit deliver the sender's mental information to your third chakra via the streams. Spend a couple minutes accepting this data.

Next, request that the Spirit use the healing streams to lift this information into your fifth chakra. The streams will now transform the psychic data into clairaudient information.

You might be able to hear this information internally or externally. Then again, third chakra data is hard to hear—until you open your mouth and speak, sing, or chant. Take a risk. Simply open your mouth and start verbalizing the transported data. Share until the sounds run out. Then take the next step.

STEP 5: **Perform Fifth Chakra Clairaudience.**
Ask the Spirit to clear the healing streams that interconnected your third chakra with that of the sender's. It will now establish streams between your fifth chakra and the sender's fifth chakra. Tell your partner to continue concentrating on the subject while the Spirit carries your partner's thoughts from their fifth chakra into your own. At this point, you will internally or externally hear insights related to the sender's

subject. Then open your mouth and share what you are thinking or hearing.

Continue speaking until you feel complete. Then ask the Spirit to use new streams of grace to disconnect you and your partner.

STEP 6: **Share and Debrief.** Tell the sender that they can open their eyes while you do the same. Discuss the interaction with the sender. What was their topic? What were they feeling, sensing, or thinking about when they were concentrating on the subject material? What points did you make that seemed accurate to them? Had you captured any exact words, phrases, or thoughts? Specifically discuss the differences that both of you perceived between the third chakra and the fifth chakra information. How were the flows of data different or similar? Interact until you both feel complete with the discussion.

STEP 7: **Close.** Thank your partner for participating and part ways.

Spiritual Telepathy
SPEAKING GOODNESS ALOUD

We are not alone. The love, support, and advice of a vast array of once-living and otherworldly spiritual beings is always available. Included in this grouping are angels, deceased masters, avatars, gurus, saints, and many other heavenly forces and forms.

The main way that these high beings present revelation is through our seventh chakra, the center of spiritual empathy. I also use the term "prophecy" to describe this gift, which is the ability to understand the Spirit's wishes for self or another. The seventh chakra is also a conduit for energies from the chakras that lie above the head.

These chakras are described in many of my books, including the first book in this series, *Subtle Energy Techniques*. You can see them on the following page's figure 2. In a nutshell, however, the three transcendent chakras that most frequently interconnect with our seventh chakra are the eighth chakra, which manages our interdimensional connections; the ninth chakra, which enables us to harmonize with others; and our eleventh chakra, through which we can direct natural and supernatural energies. I am mentioning these out-of-body chakras because I want you to understand the true significance of the seventh chakra. It is command central for all spiritual activities. Because of its range, it can be especially beneficial to transform the messages that it gathers into clairaudient insights.

Directionally, the seventh chakra sends its empathically received information into the fifth chakra through the

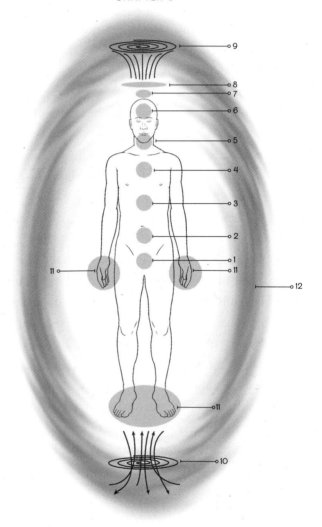

FIGURE 2: *The Twelve-Chakra System*

sixth chakra. Your sixth chakra is home to clairvoyance, or psychic visioning. Of course, you can access clairvoyant information as a stand-alone. I reveal how to do this in my book *Awaken Clairvoyant Energy*, which is the second book in this series. But sometimes, in the course of performing spiritual telepathy, a few visions are caught up in the process. Because of this, I'll show you how to unwrap a psychic vision, if one is present, in exercise 14.

It's of no small consequence to verbalize a spiritual message, whether or not it contains a clairvoyant kernel. Years ago I came upon a street fight in a gang-infested area of town. Two teenagers were circling each other with broken glass bottles. I immediately felt energy flow from my seventh chakra through my sixth and into my fifth chakra. I visualized the two boys dead, even though they had just started to cut each other. This image showed me the potential outcome of the fight. I then sensed the Spirit prompting me to open my mouth and speak—so I did.

"What would your mothers say?" I yelled.

The boys dropped the glass bottles. I was as surprised as they were. A moment later, the police arrived.

As you can see, words are powerful vehicles for delivering spiritual messages, and the following exercise will help you create those types of potent words. Specifically, it will guide you to connect with an angel.

Speaking to an Angel

All high-level beings are available through your seventh chakra, but angels are arguably the most available. They assist people of all cultures and backgrounds through their direct connection with the Spirit.

In this exercise you will be guided to connect with an angel and transform the awareness received into a telepathic message. You can also link with any other type of spiritual being by substituting the phrase "spiritual being" wherever you spot the word "angel."

As for the angels, there are many types. Each grouping is charged with a different mission, as per the following list:

- *Archangels:* Manage different realms of existence for the Spirit, such as healing, defeating evil, delivering messages, creating love, and more. They operate like "committee heads," each supervising a flight of angels.

- *Cherubim:* Winged creatures with a thousand eyes, cherubim can see and fulfill the Spirit's will and reveal your best choices.
- *Seraphim:* Beings with six wings that cleanse us and return us to holiness.
- *Shining Ones:* Beings of light that bring heavenly energies to earth.
- *Powers:* Darkly colored angels that release the earth from darkness and evil.

Is there a specific type of angel you'd like to confer with? Do you want to see which type shows up in response to a burning concern? In this exercise you can follow either option. Because the message might include the nubbins of a psychic vision, I'll show you how to accommodate your sixth chakra as well.

STEP 1: **Prepare.** Settle into a comfortable space. Focus on the particular type of angel you'd like to connect with or a subject that could benefit from angelic assistance.

STEP 2: **Conduct Spirit-to-Spirit.** Acknowledge your personal spirit, the spirits of all beneficial beings attending you, and the Spirit. Then breathe deeply and relax.

Step 3: **Create Your Connection.** Concentrate on
the angel that comes into your presence. You will
most likely sense or feel its grandeur, power, and
beauty. Now qualify the source. as you've been
taught to do in previous chapters. If you want,
you can return to the provided outline of angels
and simply ask, "Are you an archangel, cherubim,
seraphim, shining one, or power?" The correct answer will light up your body, and you'll
sense the accuracy. There are angels that don't
appear on this list, too. If the list of angels doesn't
seem right, ask the angel to reveal itself to you
through awareness or an image.

Step 4: **Receive the Spiritual Message.** Ask the
angel to transfer its message into your seventh
chakra through streams of grace, gathering
energy from the transcendent chakras as well.
Now give permission for this collected data to
be carried into your fifth chakra as if in a water-
fall of light.

Step 5: **Unpack the Message.** First, ask the angel
to separate any visual energy from the spiritual

data waiting to be assessed. If there is a visual acorn within the divine energy, ask the angel to portray it as an image on your inner mind screen. Evaluate the colors, shapes, and visuals and consider what they mean for you. You can always ask the angel to grant additional visions. If there isn't an image that appears, simply forgo this part of the step.

Then ask the angel to transform the spiritual energy within your fifth chakra into a telepathic message. You might internally or externally hear a sound, song, statement, refrain, or other verbalization. You might want to open your mouth and allow the energy to be expressed. Flow with the process until you are clear about the spiritual insight. You can ask questions of the angel as long as you desire.

STEP 6: **Finalize and Close.** When you feel complete, thank the Spirit, the angel, and all the helpers for their assistance, and return to your life.

Questions for Assessing a Clairaudient Communication

The following questions can be added to those you've been collecting from previous chapters. These relate to the formation of telepathic messages from empathically sourced data.

- Should I change a physically empathic or primal sensation into a telepathic message?

- Should I transform an empathically sensed feeling into telepathic knowledge?

- Should I shift a mental knowing into a telepathic awareness?

- Should I turn a spiritual revelation into a telepathic message?

- If the above includes a clairvoyant image, what is that image?

· · · · · · ·
Summary

There are four types of telepathy, the term defined as the transference of thoughts, passions, feelings, and awareness into the fifth chakra in order to gain a verbal understanding. These four styles involve turning information obtained through primal/physical, feeling, mental, and spiritual empathy into telepathic messages. The latter category can also involve the assessment of a clairvoyant image delivered through spiritual energy.

CHAPTER SEVEN

Natural Clairaudience

COMMUNING
WITH NATURE

Every so often my dog Honey shows up in a dream barking. He does this when I'm out of town. You see, when I'm home he wakes me at 4 a.m. to go outside. I suppose he doesn't see any reason to stop prompting me into action just because I'm traveling.

Clairaudience is one of the most enjoyable and productive tools for communicating with beings from nature, and not only our companion animals. There are nearly infinite types of natural beings, including beings from this earth and other planets, constellations, and dimensions. After briefly describing a few of these different sources, I'll organize them in two basic categories: earthly and otherworldly. I'll then walk you through two exercises.

The first exercise will link you with beings of the earth, such as animals and plants, as well as fantastical beings, such as unicorns and fairies. The second exercise will throw open the universal door and enable connection with sources as far-flung as off-world aliens. Two additional tips will bolster the exercises and your ability to communicate with nature.

Beings of Nature
THE DIVERSITY AROUND YOU

Our ancestors knew that nature teems with conscious beings. They understood that a rock can project a personality as strong as a person's and that a talented shaman can be equally conversant in the languages of trolls, Plutonians, and daffodils. These spiritually aware shamans, intuitives, and healers assumed that natural beings could interconnect across time and space, and that a gifted intuitive could request information and healing from a variety of multidimensional beings, whether they occupied the past, present, or future.

Whether or not they consciously knew it, our nature-based ancestors employed their tenth chakra to commune with the living world. As shown on figure 2 on page 202, this energy center located under the feet connects us all to the environment. Unfortunately, over the centuries we have forgotten how to talk with natural beings, restricting our conversations to other humans. Even then, they—

we—haven't done a very good job at corresponding truthfully or openly. What if we decided to return to our earlier interactions, relating to the amazing array of natural beings, whether they are living or deceased? Think of how much we could learn—and become.

We're already almost completely dependent on the environment and natural beings. We are part of the skein of animals, plants, trees, and stars, while natural elements compose every part of our body. For example, recent research suggests that our bodies rely on sunlight, even absorbing it during our earliest of embryonic stages through the melanin and neuromelanin to form pathways for our energetic and physical body (Bynum 2012, 4).

As well, thousands of medicines are plant derivatives, with about 80 percent of the world's people employing herbs as their main medicines and about 40 percent of the medicines used in the United States made of plant spin-offs (Medicine Hunter, n.d.). There are other sorts of medicines, however—ones that we can draw upon through physical and subtle processes.

For instance, a cat's purr improves bone density and also helps heal tendons and ligaments (Lyons 2003). A dog's saliva contains proteins that heal wounds twice as fast than if the injury was left alone, and some types of snake venom dissolve blood clots (Goodnet, n.d.).

How about our winged friends? The presence of birds alleviates symptoms of dementia in the elderly, reducing agitation and confusion (ASA Staff, n.d.). And reptiles aren't to be left out. In fact, scientists have figured out that certain types of frog skin contain antimicrobial peptides, which enhance wound healing (Advanced Tissue, n.d.).

To me, the most exciting application of these and other discoveries related to nature is the exponential gains we can create through clairaudience. We don't have to spread our skin with frog peptides or actually pet a cat to reap the gains. Clairaudience is a vibrational activity. By sensing or "hearing" a frog, cat, tree, or any other being, we reap all the benefits I've just outlined, plus so many more.

I've actually used clairaudience to connect with—and learn from—hundreds of different nature beings. For example, I once worked with a natural medicine healer in the Amazonian basin who grows all the medicinal plants of that particular Peruvian region on his land.

One day I wandered the farm with him. Using my empathic skills and clairaudience, which you learned about in the last chapter, I only had to touch a plant to hear it "talk." It was as if my inner self could translate plant language. For their part, the plants were delighted to tell me the services they could perform for humans. Examples included alleviating nausea, healing wounds, and blocking the spread of cancer cells. In every case, the shaman told me I was accurate.

There are beings beyond those on earth, however. During the same trip to Peru, I was awakened one night by a star being. It shared a song of love and beauty. The next day, the shaman told me that I had once lived on the Blue Planet, as had he, and he'd also been visited by this being.

"Why do these beings bother with us immature humans?" I wondered.

"Because we are all of the same family," the being said.

And so we are—every plant, animal, rock, and star, including fantasy characters.

As you'll determine in this chapter, you can communicate with all "normal" earthly beings, whether alive or deceased, but also fantastical earthly beings. I remember when a client brought her son in to see me. He was five or six and had huge blue glasses, which he insisted on wearing even when asleep or in the bathtub. His mother was beside herself. If she forced him to remove them, he'd scream at the top of his lungs and shut his eyes, refusing to open them until his glasses were back on.

I asked his mother to leave the office and asked the boy what he could see with his glasses on. He blinked and answered.

"Dragons," he replied.

"Can you only see them with your eyeglasses on?" I asked.

"No," he admitted. "I can see dragons no matter what. I can only HEAR them with my glasses on."

For some reason, this precious child had always been able to see dragons with his psychic and visible eyes. And then, one day, he could hear them. Because it was the same day on which he put his first set of eyeglasses on his nose, he decided that the glasses were key to his clairaudience. It took a couple of sessions, but I was able to show him that he could communicate with the dragons without eyeglasses. You see, he was clairaudient. As we worked together, I encouraged him to write books about his dragons so as to best use his gift. Some day these books might make it into the hands of children everywhere.

How do we communicate with all these natural beings, from plants to dragons? From a quantum perspective, subtle energy interconnects everything and everyone across time and space. In order to relate to a natural being—alive or dead, earthly or otherworldly, normal or fantastical— we've only to use our clairaudience.

While there are limitless numbers of natural beings, there are two basic categories. Knowing about these groups can help you qualify natural sources and direct questions to the correct beings.

Major Types of Natural Beings

There are two main categories of natural beings: earthly and otherworldly. Within the earthly category are everyday and fantastical beings. Everyday earthly beings include your house pets, plants, and flowers. Fantastical earthly beings are whimsical and usually known about through legends. These include fairies, dragons, and griffons, to name a few. Otherworldly natural beings are from non-earth planets, spaces, and places.

That's about as straightforward as these categories get. Within each distinction are beings that might be living or deceased or dwell in the past, current time period, concurrent reality, and possible future. There are beings that are immaterial and material—and sometimes natural beings that can be a little of everything.

I have a perfect example.

For years, my family has owned dogs named Honey, all male golden retrievers. The first Honey, which I'll call Honey I, lived a generation back. I raised my sons with

Honey II, who died a few years ago. A couple of years after his passing, I heard a voice.

"I'm coming back." That voice was Honey II.

After Honey II told me he was going to incarnate again soon, I was bombarded with signs of and dreams about honey nectar and also tanks—G.I. Joe tanks, Sherman tanks, toilet tanks, and more. The latter only made sense when my son found an image of a puppy on the internet named Tank. He declared that this was Honey. Tank soon became Honey III. Shortly after Honey III arrived, he went through all the health crises that had taken out Honey II. This time, however, Honey survived.

I believe that all the Honeys are the same soul. Honey is most obviously a natural earthly being when in his living dog form, but he can also speak when he's deceased. I've known Honey as material and immaterial, and who knows what concurrent reality he was hanging out in between reincarnations? On top of that, after Honey II died, I asked him who or what he really was. That night I had a dream. In it I perceived Honey's soul as a huge cloaked figure. He shared that he was a master from a different dimension. I do have to say that he is one of the wisest and most fun-loving beings I've ever met.

The two exercises in this chapter will provide you slightly different ways to connect with beings from the two overarching categories and cope with the blurring between lines. Now have fun exploring the basic subsets of natural beings.

Natural Earthly Beings

The following beings, whether everyday or fantastical, originate on earth. I have listed the most basic categories and provided a few insights about what you can gain by connecting with members of each.

Everyday Beings

You can connect with the following everyday beings, whether they are deceased or alive:

ANIMALS: Mammals can grant insight, warnings, protection, powers, healing, and direction. In fact, each species is bestowed with certain abilities that they can lend or teach us. Besides delivering specific healing energies, dogs provide companionship, cats represent individuality, and bears symbolize strength. You don't have to be in the presence of an animal to benefit from its healing powers. You can request that a dog lick you ethereally to assist with wound healing.

BIRDS: Birds show which direction to take or avoid. As well, their songs provide vibrational healing and deliver spiritual messages.

INSECTS: Insects point out details. For instance, an ant can indicate what burden to carry or set down. A buzzing mosquito can reveal a "stinging" person or situation.

REPTILES: Reptiles represent transformation and reveal shadow issues. If a snake shows up in real life or a dream, you'll want to ask it what you must shed or how you need to change.

AMPHIBIANS: Water is the medium of amphibians and symbolizes emotions and intuition. If a frog hops into your world, ask what intuitive leaps you need to make.

Plants, Trees, and Flowers

The greenery of this good earth is a vital source of information, inspiration, and medical data. Following are a few of the blessings we can access from this grouping through clairaudience.

PLANTS: This category includes plants in general, from algae to shrubbery. Each specific species generates physical and subtle energies that are curative. Plants are also aware of the environment and can clue us in to weather patterns and other environmental shifts.

TREES: Each tree species engenders its own medicinal properties and also conveys additional vital information. Science is just beginning to remember the holistic nature of trees, as is being revealed through the research wing of the HeartMath Institute, which has been monitoring the circadian rhythms and electrical patterns of trees. To date, early results are suggesting that the electrical activity of trees is intertwined with the patterns of the sun, moon, stones, and earth. We can monitor tree activity and predict upcoming weather patterns, such as impending earthquakes. It also seems that trees respond to human emotions (HeartMath Institute 2016). I personally find that trees can also illuminate someone's true nature, connect a person to the Spirit, and provide soothing and calming energies.

FLOWERS: Every blossom holds data deposited in
it by birds, bees, and other messengers. You can
retrieve this information and find out the secrets
of nature. Poetry and songs also emanate from
flowers, and every type of flower species generates unique vibrations that can attune a person
to a specific psychological and physical concern.

Natural Elements

Elements compose every aspect of physical reality. Subtle
elements are tiny versions of the basic elements, such as
fire and wood, and make up the subtle universe.

You can communicate with the beings attached to the
various subtle elements. Called elementals, they are char-
acterized by the same features as their corresponding elements, which they can summon, organize, dissipate, and
eliminate. The easiest way to connect and communicate
with an elemental is through your clairaudience. (More
information about elements is available in the first book
of this series, *Subtle Energy Techniques*.)

Snapshots follow that describe what each element provides and how each elemental can assist you.

- **Earth Element:** Protection, groundedness, and
repair.

- **Wood Element:** Rebirth, vision, purpose, and new direction.

- **Air Element:** Transmission of ideas, data, and mentality.

- **Metal Element:** Deflection of negativity and transmission of spiritual messages.

- **Fire Element:** Power, passion, purging, and vivacity.

- **Water Element:** Intuition, emotions, and flow.

- **Stone Element:** Stones hold historical knowledge and can direct energy, depending on their type. For instance, water stones remember everything that has occurred in a streambed. Clear crystals hold spiritual ideas, and amethyst repels evil and attracts goodness.

- **Light Element:** Every color of light is carried on—and reflects—a specific type of data. A splash or beam of light can inform and instruct but also provide specific types of healing and manifesting. For instance, blue is calming, red ignites passion, and white purifies and sanctifies.

- **Sound Element:** All sounds deliver vibrational power and encourage change. You can always ask to communicate with the sound elements related to the chakra tones taught in chapter 2.

- **Ether Element:** Consciousness, wisdom, and transformation.
- **Star Element:** Star energies are composed of fire and ether. As such, they ignite consciousness and higher principles.

What might an elemental confer through clairaudience? During a sojourn to Wales a few years ago, I "heard" a set of stone elementals calling me from a field I was driving by. The sounds were like a whisper, which I could interpret with my inner mind. I pulled off the road, and my friends and I sat in the field, listening to the stones.

They conveyed stories about the various communities that had occupied that land, including people and animals. They also shared stories from the stars, telling of the beginning of the cosmos and the Creator. My inner fifth chakra self simply translated the stone elemental language into my own, and I knew without a doubt that the words being pasted together were accurate.

A few days later, I was hiking up a cliff not far away from the stone field. The path was narrow. Near the top, the wind began wrapping around me. I felt frightened. Would it push me off the mountain? Instead, the wind seemed to guide me to a cave at the top of the cliff. There I "heard" the wind elementals remind me about a life I had led in this very place. At the end of that life, in which I was killed defending my people, I returned to my soul form and ran with the wind elementals for a while. Remembering all of this through the assistance of the air elementals in the cave reminded me that I had nothing to fear from death. That was an important message, as my father was dying from lung cancer at the time.

Fantastical Earthly Beings

The earthly realm has existed for a long time and evolved over several epochs. At different times, the earth has been occupied by beings that most of us only know about through myths and legends, such as dragons and trolls. I believe that these beings lived on this earth in earlier eras and that many still occupy this land, though in a different dimension.

I've connected with various fantastical beings since I was a child. When I was young, I talked with fairies and a unicorn would appear in my dreams, instructing me on higher matters. As an adult I was able to hear dragons for a couple of years. They revealed different ways to employ my spiritual powers.

In the next listing, I organize the main groups of earthly fantastical beings as per their relationship with four of the major elements—earth, water, fire, and air. Know that while I put fairies and dragons under "sylphs," which are air beings, there are fairies and dragons associated with all elements and aspects of life. No matter what other element the fairies and dragons interact with, however, they always relate to air because they fly.

Gnomes/Earth Dwellers

Gnomes are earth dwellers. There are many types of gnomes, each of which relates to a specific vibratory band of the earth, such as stones, gems, metals, and minerals. Gnomes will build houses specific to their vibratory rates, such as with alabaster, iron, marble, or the like. Most are smaller than human beings, but some can be as large as giants.

Clairaudient communication with a gnome will enable you to command magic. However, never turn the magic against a gnome or it will turn on you.

These earth dwellers can conduct the following tasks:

PYGMIES: Work with stones, gems, and metals and help you find lost treasures.

DWARVES: Assist you in getting work done and
unearthing knowledge from previous earth
epochs.

TREE AND FOREST SPRITES: Also called devas, these
live in or attend the trees, plants, and regions
of wooded areas. Specific types include the
following:

Brownies or Elves: These bearded beings are
twelve to eighteen inches tall. They can
maneuver the invisible worlds and help
you do the same upon request. (The
females don't have beards.)

Pixies: Pranksters that reveal what is hidden.

Leprechauns: Pagan cobblers. If you find their
wealth, they will give you three wishes.

Dryads: Spirits that live in the trees. There
are specific types as well. For instance,
the Meliades are nymphs of the fruit trees;
the Daphaie are nymphs of the laurel trees.

Green Man: An ancient deity representing
the union between humans and nature.
Links you to the Divine Masculine.

Green Lady: Partner to the Green Man.
Links you to the Divine Feminine.

Undines/Water Beings

Water elementals can be consulted about your own or others' emotions and for intuitive advice. They also help create beauty. Most undines resemble humans but are more ethereal, taking on the characteristics of the lakes, spray, oceans, or whichever body of water they occupy. Names include the water sprites, sea maids, and mermaids. As well, there are nereids, which are tall nymphs, and limoniades, which are small nymphs that live off flowers.

Salamanders/Fire Activators

Nothing can come alive without the salamanders, as they activate life energy. Salamanders can be summoned through smoke, fire, or vapors. Some look like small balls of light; others appear as large and glowing spheres. The Djin is their ruler and can grant wishes or help you meet your goals.

Sylphs/Air Beings

Considered sacred, air is within everything. The most famous air beings are the fairies, which can sculpt the snowflakes, clouds, plants, and flowers. Fairies live hundreds of years and are really the magical gardeners of nature. Fairies can also assume human form, but only for a while. Specific types of fairies and other air beings include:

WILL-O'-WISP: Rare fairies that travel in fog and appear as flickering lights. If asked politely, they will tell you a truth.

PEAT FAIRIES: Mud-covered fairies that deliver ill will on the lazy.

UNICORNS: White horse-like beings with magical horns. They dwelled in Lemuria and Atlantis, ancient human societies that are described in the next section. Unicorns can connect you to other realms, provide healing, and forgive evil. Their horn is made of stardust. If they sprinkle you with the dust, consider yourself blessed.

SIDHE: A supernatural fairy race that grants wishes. I believe that they are the same as the shining ones, angels that I described in the last chapter.

PERIS: Fairies descended from spirits denied paradise. They can tell you if your efforts will produce good or evil.

CENTAURS: Beings with a human torso and horse body that advise on warriorism and nobility.

POOKAS: Fairies that live near ancient stones and convey ancient information.

HIPPOGRIFFS: Winged horses with the upper bodies of eagles that can transport you to other realms.

DRAGONS: There are many types of these winged beings. They can fly, breathe fire or other elements, and travel the magical lands. If they choose, they can help dreams come true and reveal hidden treasures.

GENIES: Bring luck and wealth.

GRIFFINS: Flying beings that blend eagle and lion traits and can help you journey to various time zones.

LIGHT ELVES: Fairies in charge of light and rainbows.

Otherworldly Natural Beings

This category is more complicated than it might seem at first blush. Technically, it features natural beings from non-Earth worlds and dimensions. Sometimes we call members of this community *extraterrestrials*, which means "non-earthlings" or "aliens." You can potentially connect with otherworldly beings that come from this or other galaxies.

One of my first experiences with aliens occurred years ago when I was invited to watch several mediums channel extraterrestrials (ETs). As the ETs entered the channels' bodies, the hosts' voices changed. Their bodies appeared bigger and their voices fell in pitch. When the process was finished, the ETs exited and the hosts' souls returned. Their bodies shook and then deflated. Their voices rose in pitch, and the channelers were so tired that they had to eat immediately.

The ETs' messages were beautiful, composed of pleas for peace. The entire experience left me worried about the effects of full transmediumship on a channel's body, however, which is one of the reasons I offered protection techniques in chapter 3.

The otherworldly category is actually quite complex. For one, certain types of otherworldly beings inhabit or once inhabited Earth, though they originally came from somewhere else. The following list hints at a few of these alien kingdoms. The other complication is that many of us are probably descendants of interplanetary beings and perhaps even angels, which I consider divine, not natural, beings. In fact, many of the cultures I've studied or interacted with believe that their ancestors came from other planets and settled on Earth. For example, some Cherokee tribes state that they came from the Pleiades, and the African Dogons believe they are descended from an interplanetary race from the Sirius star system.

The biblical book of Genesis presents a story that fits with this assumption, sharing that the Nephilim mated with humans to produce the "Giants in the Earth," or tall and strong people. Many people believe that the Nephilim were fallen angels; still others assert that they were extraterrestrials. If you have alien or angelic blood, it could be relatively easy for you to link with these beings and use clairaudience to communicate and also activate genetically bestowed spiritual gifts.

Following is an outline of the major types of otherworldly beings I've connected with or know that others are familiar with.

AGHARIANS: Asiatic or Nordic humans, originally alien, who established a kingdom under the Gobi Desert thousands of years ago. Some people believe that they still live there. Connect with them to learn about magic and cosmological history.

ANAKIM: Descendants of the "Giants in the Earth," who were birthed by intercourse between the Nephilim, or fallen angels/aliens, and earth women. It is said that they currently live in cavern systems under Africa and other areas. From these sites they conduct interstellar flights. Connect with them to activate your spiritual powers and warrior abilities, undergo soul journeys, and activate any gifts inherited through your bloodline.

ANDROMEDANS: An extraterrestrial council that keeps track of all aliens living on or off this planet, whether they are well-intentioned or not. You can connect with this council to get suggestions about which beings to interact with or to qualify a being that has contacted you.

ANUNNAKI: Aliens from the Nibiru planet that served as deities in ancient Mesopotamia. Some experts equate them with the Nephilim. Interact with the positive members of this race to learn how to use power wisely.

ARCTURIANS: The most advanced civilization in our galaxy. Arcturians can raise your vibrational level to that of love and help you use subtle energies wisely.

ATLANTEANS: On earth, this ancient civilization was known for its advanced energy technology, levitating objects and directing power through crystals. I believe that they once inhabited the Pleiades and brought this technology, including faster-than-light travel, to Earth from their home planet. Some people believe that they still live underground on Earth.

DRACONIANS: Reptilian (or negative) aliens from Alpha Draconis that are attempting to take over the earth. Some are disguised as humans and aim for leadership positions so they can cause evil and destruction. You don't need to deliberately speak with them, but it's important to know about their existence because you don't want to be fooled by—or connect with—a Draconian if you can help it. If we know that a certain type of being exists, we can avoid being manipulated. In general, manipulative beings, whether physical or subtle in form, will create an upset stomach, a churning sensation, or extreme hot and cold. Ask for protection from the Spirit if something like this occurs.

GREYS: Group of extraterrestrials that feed off human and animal fluids and abduct people. You don't want to contact them. Just know that they exist, for the same reason that you want to know about Draconians. If physical or emotional upsets alert you to the presence of a Grey, simply ask the Spirit for cleansing and protection.

LEMURIANS: Members of a "lost land" on Earth that were originally from the Pleiades. In fact, I believe that they are related to the original off-world Atlanteans but came to Earth before the Atlanteans did. The Lemurians lived in concert with the land. Most likely, many indigenous communities are descendants of the Lemurians. Communicate with them to bond with any natural being and volunteer as a peacemaker.

LYRANS: Inhabitants of what is probably the first planet inhabited by human beings. I equate this planet with the Garden of Eden. Communicate with them for knowledge of good and evil and other spiritual matters.

NEPHILIM: Group of winged beings that are either fallen angels or beings from Orion that inexcusably mated with Earth women to create the Giants and their descendants, the Anakim. The "good" Anakim may have helped humans evolve, showing them how to build the pyramids, cook with fire, and perform healing. The evil Anakim became a set of ruling Aryans, cold, hard, and cruel. Connect with the positive beings to gain keen insight and help. If you believe you carry

Nephilim blood, ask the beneficial Nephilim to activate your powers for beneficial reasons.

ORIONS: Beings from the Orion Belt. Some are noble and some are untrustworthy but all hold knowledge about infinity and the Creator.

PLEIADIANS: Multidimensional beings originally from the Pleiadian stars. Some came to this planet thousands of years ago to create the Lemurian and Atlantean civilizations. They can teach you about your divine nature.

SIRIANS: Beings from Sirius that taught the Mayans, African Dogons, and Egyptians. They can provide data about math, astronomy, time, and other advanced knowledge.

Now it's time to connect with both earthly and otherworldly natural beings, which you'll learn how to do in the next two exercises.

Exercise
—15—

Communicating with Natural Earthly Beings

Do you want to connect with an everyday or a fantastical natural being or leave the choice to the Spirit? Maybe you have a specific being in mind, such as a house pet or a tree from your backyard. Maybe you feel called to discuss life matters with a fairy or dragon. Or maybe you want to see what the Spirit blows in.

This exercise will use a blend of clairaudient empathy and channeling. Why empathy? Natural beings are very emotive and sensory based, so it's important to relate to them via the empathic abilities we explored in the last chapter. As you learned, empathic sensations can be transformed into clairaudient sounds, and this is the process you'll employ in the following exercise. Many natural beings are also quite heart-based; the heart is located in the fourth chakra and is the center of higher emotional connections and healing. Know that you might be quite aware of your heart during an interaction with a natural earthly being.

STEP 1: **Prepare.** Find a quiet place in which to concentrate or choose a place in nature that will support your connection to a natural being, whether it's earthly or fantastical. You might already have an earthly being in mind; focus on that being or an important topic.

STEP 2: **Conduct Spirit-to-Spirit.** Affirm your own spirit and the helping spirits. If you're already thinking about a specific spirit, affirm its spirit. Then acknowledge the presence of the Spirit in its most natural form. Some people use the word Creator to describe the Spirit in the context of the natural world.

STEP 3: **Connect.** Clear your mind and ask the Spirit to forge healing streams between you and the natural being you are to interact with. These streams will serve as pathways of communication between you and that being. On your part, they will link to your empathic chakras, including your heart chakra as well as your fifth chakra. If the Spirit connects this being to your seventh chakra, you might also find your sixth or visual chakra involved with your communication.

Now qualify the source using the techniques
you've already been working with in this book.
What type of natural being is it? Is it an earthly
or fantastical being? Do you already have (or
have you had) an association with this being or
not? Ask all the questions that make sense to ask,
and then request that the Spirit help this being
send you a message.

STEP 4: **Receive and Interpret the Message.**
Because you've interconnected empathically,
any of your empathic chakras might perceive
a message. You might be struck with a physical sensation (first chakra), an emotion (second
chakra), an idea (third chakra), a spiritual knowing (seventh chakra), or even a clairvoyant image
(sixth chakra via the seventh chakra). Your heart
might also open you to a feeling of love. All
these empathically received energies will flow
to your fifth chakra, and the Spirit or another
higher source will transform them into verbal
information. Your fifth chakra will also directly
hear from the natural being and note internal or
external sounds. Ask any questions you'd like and
continue to interrelate.

STEP 5: **Close.** When you sense that your communication is complete, ask the Spirit to help you lovingly disconnect from the natural being. Streams of grace provide each of you what is needed, and you can return to your everyday life when you're ready.

Additional Tip

COMMUNICATING WITH A FAMILY PET

Each animal species has its own language, and all animals have a fifth chakra through which they can translate your message into their personal language. You have to conduct the communiqué with a genuine heartfelt emotion, however, so they can receive it. Pets are love-based and will most easily link with you through an already established heart/fourth chakra bond.

You can start your interaction for two reasons. Maybe your animal has been acting differently or speaking verbally and you'd like to understand what's happening. Or you might desire to send them a message. The instructions work either way.

If your animal has been communicating at you, ask the Spirit to bring its message through your empathic centers and into your fifth chakra, where the Spirit will translate that energy into verbally understood information.

To send a message, concentrate on your heart and your love for the animal. Then create a statement in your mind (fifth chakra) and either think it or say it aloud. Ask the Spirit to send that message through your heart chakra to the animal's fifth chakra. You can also picture, sense, feel, and think about that message. You can continue with this back-and-forth flow as long as you desire.

Exercise
--16--

Connecting with Otherworldly Beings

This exercise is intended to help you communicate with an otherworldly being. This being might already have reached out to you; either that or it will show up during the exercise in response to your focus. To conduct it, you'll combine guided writing and receptive channeling.

What kind of help can an otherworldly being provide? Just about anything. Review the list provided in the section "Otherworldly Natural Beings" earlier in this chapter to check their individual expertise.

For example, I once worked with a client who had a chronic autoimmune dysfunction. Who showed up to share data and healing but a Nephilim? Declaring that it was one of my client's long-ago ancestors, the Nephilim stated that my client had unconsciously rejected her alien genetics as being evil. However, this Nephilim ancestor, which had begun its earthly interactions as an evil being, had evolved and could now stimulate the genetics that could heal my client. The Nephilim did this—and over the next six months, my client's illness slowly disappeared.

With this story in mind, get ready to let a cosmic connection make a real difference in your life.

STEP 1: **Prepare.** Settle into a quiet area with writing instruments. Choose an issue, concern, or opportunity you'd like to focus on and frame it into a statement. Write this statement down.

STEP 2: **Conduct Spirit-to-Spirit.** Affirm your personal spirit, others' spirits, and the Spirit.

STEP 3: **Request an Otherworldly Helper.** Ask that Spirit adjust your brain state so you can connect with an otherworldly being that can benefit you. One might appear that you've already met before or the Spirit will assign a new one.

STEP 4: **Assess the Being.** Who or what has appeared? Where are they from? Ask the Spirit, your gatekeeper, or some other trusted source— such as the Andromedans, who regulate on- and off-world aliens—to assess this being for you. Is it to be trusted? Is this a Spirit-approved source? Let the Spirit provide you clairaudient insights until you feel safe with this being.

STEP 5: **Relate to the Otherworldly Being.** Grab your writing instruments and ask questions to enable a flow of written communication. I recommend that you employ receptive channeling, asking questions like the following:

- Where are you from?
- When did/do/will you exist?
- Can you describe your features to me?
- Can you show me an image, if it's appropriate?
- What is the reason that the Spirit has assigned you to me?
- What is the message you need to deliver?
- What else do I need to know?
- If I need to follow up with you, how can I do so?

Spend a few more minutes asking all other pertinent questions, and then write a summary about what you've learned.

STEP 6: **Close.** When ready, ask the Spirit to release the otherworldly being and use healing streams to rebalance yourself. Return to your everyday life when you're ready.

Additional Tip

WORKING THE EIGHTH AND TENTH CHAKRAS

In the first book in the Essential Energy Library series (of which this is the third book), I introduced you to five chakras beyond the seven in-body chakras. Two of these are especially useful to work with when connecting with natural beings, whether they are earthly or otherworldly.

The tenth chakra is found about two feet underneath your feet (see figure 2 on page 202). It mainly accesses your physical body through your bones. The tenth chakra links you to all earthly connections and keeps you grounded while you're acting clairaudiently.

Your eighth chakra is located a few inches above your head and is anchored in the thymus (see figure 2). It regulates mystical connections and can enhance your ability to bond with fantastical earthly and otherworldly beings across all time periods.

* * * *

Here is how to more clearly perceive—and be safe in—the presence of any type of natural being. While conducting Spirit-to-Spirit in either of the two exercises in this chapter, also ask the Spirit to send healing streams upward through your tenth chakra. These streams will flow into your feet and upward through all your bones, nourishing your entire body elementally. This stream will continue to move beyond the top of your head and keep your entire energetic and physical system clear while you are interacting clairaudiently. You can run this elemental stream during an entire clairaudient session.

If you are linking with an otherworldly being, you can add an additional step. First, set up the tenth chakra stream of energy. Then, while conducting Spirit-to-Spirit in exercise 16, let the tenth chakra stream of energy momentarily pause and percolate in your eighth chakra. This action will bolster your energetic field and serve as a radar for beings from the farthest regions of time and space. Then continue with step 4, "Assess the Being," and the rest of the exercise.

When closing, know that the Spirit will readjust all your chakras through healing streams. You are now more than ready for our final sojourn into clairaudience. It's time to adapt clairaudience to healing and manifesting.

Questions for Assessing a Clairaudient Communication

You can add these questions to the list you are developing throughout this book's progression.

- Am I in contact with a natural being or should I be?

- What type of natural being am I communicating with or should I contact?

  ★ earthly

    – *everyday*
    – *fantastical*

  ★ otherworldly

· · · · · ·
Summary

Clairaudience is an ideal method for interacting with natural beings, of which there are two main varieties. One category consists of earthly beings, which are subdivided into everyday and fantastical beings. Besides interacting with earthly beings, you can also converse with otherworldly beings, such as beings from other planets or dimensions. All in all, there is much more to this world than you might have thought.

CHAPTER EIGHT

Healing and Manifesting Through Clairaudience

I once asked a friend who is the chief executive officer of a large company to describe his job. He was acquainted with energy medicine, so I was interested in hearing what he might say.

"Healing and manifesting," he said. "That's all I ever really do…that's all any of us do," he added.

Bottom line, the application of all our spiritual gifts, including clairaudience, reduces to healing or manifesting. Healing involves releasing energy that isn't beneficial and might even be harmful. Manifesting is the other side of the coin and occurs when we attract what we need. Can you think of any aspect of life that *doesn't* involve one or both of these activities?

In this context, clairaudience is the peanut butter between the two slices of bread that are healing and manifesting. It is a vehicle for figuring out what to release and how best to do so. It is also the mechanism for determining what you need and how to acquire it. You'll learn how to perform both maneuvers in this chapter, which features two foundational exercises.

The first exercise outlines an easy way to release energy, and the second exercise promotes attracting your desires. You can always use both exercises together, first performing a healing and then opening to a manifestation, as we must usually let go of what's unnecessary to make room for something new. Additional tips will serve as a special bonus for applying this material.

Exercise
--17--

Healing Through Clairaudience

Are you ready to deploy your clairaudience to release harmful or unnecessary energies? The following steps will guide you along the clairaudient path to freedom. You'll be using standard channeling of whichever nature you desire—full, partial, or receptive. Basically, you'll connect with a source that will provide information while you're wielding healing streams to create a positive shift.

STEP 1: **Prepare.** Find a quiet space in which to work and assure that you won't be disturbed. Concentrate on a situation that requires letting go of unneeded energies.

STEP 2: **Conduct Spirit-to-Spirit.** Affirm your personal spirit, the helping spirits, and the Spirit. Then ask the Spirit or your gatekeeper to assign a source that can inform you about the reason you are afflicted with negative energies. This source will be interacting with the Spirit to clear up the problem.

STEP 3: **Qualify the Source.** Sense the presence of the healing source and qualify it using the tools taught in this book. What is the source? What time period does it come from? Ask the source what type of channeling it would like to employ when you fully open to its assistance during the next step. Will it prefer receptive, partial, or full channeling?

Is that choice acceptable to you? If you'd like to utilize a different type of channeling, negotiate with the source. You might picture, hear, or sense the response. You can always double check the final decision with the Spirit, which will send you an affirmative feeling or an internally or externally heard word as to which type of channeling is best to employ. If the source won't comply with your final decision, you don't want to work with it. Ask the Spirit to send a different source and qualify it.

STEP 4: **Receive the Information.** Concentrate on the selected situation and ask the source to inform you about the cause of the problem through your selected channeling method. Ask the source whichever questions seem logical. When did the challenge ensue? What were the circumstances? Are there attachments or other energetic matters involved? The key question to conclude your interaction with is this: What wisdom can I take from this experience that will allow me to release the negative energies?

STEP 5: **Request Healing Streams.** As soon as you understand the causes of the negative energy, as well as the wisdom you can glean, ask the source to interact with the Spirit and send healing streams through you. These healing streams will clean your system—body, mind, and soul—and also remain connected as long as needed.

STEP 6: **Close.** When you feel finished, thank all
the spirits that assisted you and return to your
normal life when ready.

Additional Tip
HEALING THROUGH TONGUE SPEAKING

As implied in chapter 4, speaking in tongues can be beautifully healing, especially if you serve as a conduit for an angelic chorus. You can channel angelic healing by deliberately asking the Spirit to assign you an angel or a flight of angels to assist with your particular concern.

Return to exercise 17, Healing Through Clairaudience. When conducting Spirit-to-Spirit in step 2, specifically request that the Spirit appoint you an angel or a flight of angels to act as your source. You can review the types of angels by reviewing the list provided in exercise 14, Speaking to an Angel, on page 204.

When qualifying the angelic source, simply let the Spirit or the angel tell you more about itself. You might hear the responses internally or externally and in any sound form, such as words, song, or poetry. You might even hear an environmental noise that provides confirmation or insight.

The next step, which involves receiving the source's information, is to be accomplished through tongue speaking, specifically divine speaking. Give permission for the angelic source to send you a healing message. This communication will be wrapped within streams of grace and poured through the backside of your fifth chakra. Open your mouth and let yourself sing, state, or otherwise transmit the angelic love pouring through you. Move your body if you'd like, such as by swaying or dancing.

As the waves of sound and healing flow through the entirety of your body, the angelic vibrations gently but firmly push out the reams of negative energy, replacing them with saintly blessings. Once your body is fully saturated with love and ease, move to step 6 of exercise 17 and spend time in gratitude.

Additional Tip

REPROGRAMMING YOUR DNA WITH CLAIRAUDIENT HEALING

Can you reprogram harmful DNA through clairaudience? Yes, in accordance with research originating in Russia. Scientist Pjotr Garjajev has shown that DNA stores information like a computer does, using grammatical words and syntax. In fact, human languages might actually be verbalizations of our DNA. Moreover, spoken words and phrases can alter and rearrange DNA. To prove the point, the Russian researchers have used vibration and language on human subjects to improve their metabolism and alter speech defects. They have also changed frog embryos into salamander embryos.

According to the Russian research, the key to using sound to alter DNA is to "hypercommunicate," which involves employing sounds arrived at and accessed intuitively (Underground Health Reporter 2016). That's what we do through clairaudience.

If you need to alter your own or another's DNA, you need to connect with a powerful and spot-on source. The best place to acquire the correct sounds is from the future.

Remember, subtle energy is available from all time periods. Logically, the most powerful DNA reprogramming happens with sounds pulled from the future in which you're already healed. The purpose of this tip is to enable you to do this.

Use exercise 17, Healing Through Clairaudience, as your base. When preparing, you can either select a condition that relates to your DNA and ancestry or ask the Spirit to choose one that can be cleared up through DNA reprogramming. Next, perform step 3, Qualify the Source, but ask that the Spirit send you a messenger from the future. The featured future will be the one in which a healing has been successfully administered through clairaudient-applied DNA alteration.

Qualify the source as you normally would. Who or what is present? What type of being is it? Where is it from? When you are assured about the source, move to step 4, Receive the Information. You can open your mouth and simply allow the source to sound through you. You might hear words, phrases, or other sounds in your mind. If you can, duplicate them as closely as you can aloud. If that's impossible, listen to the sounds while the messenger sends streams of grace through your fifth chakra and the entirety of your body. Feel the shift resulting from this dynamic activity.

Ask too that the streams deliver the sequencing directly into your DNA and the chemical soup that surrounds your DNA. Called the epigenetic material, this biochemical material holds your ancestors' memories. The streams of grace carry healing not only to you but to your ancestry and progeny.

When you sense that the healing streams are fully infused, move to the closing step, step 6. With gratitude in your heart, release the messenger back to the future and return to your life when you are ready.

Manifesting Through Clairaudience

Do you want to land a desire in 3-D reality? Is there a goal you'd like to achieve? Do you want to lasso a miracle? These and a million other objectives can be the focus of clairaudient manifesting.

The following exercise is a bare-bones approach to drawing positive energies into your life using clairaudience. The ensuing additional tips will present a kaleidoscope of beneficial applications. Ideally, you will first conduct exercise 17, Healing Through Clairaudience, so your system is wide open for new energy.

STEP 1: **Prepare.** Settle into a comfortable place in which you will remain undisturbed for a few minutes. Focus on a desire or need and compose a statement describing that wish. Use present tense verbs, as you want to emphasize the fact that you are already manifesting your desire rather than waiting for it. You can create either a specific or a general request.

For instance, you can craft a detailed entreaty, such as this: "I am attracting a new job that uses all my skills and rewards me accordingly." You can also compose a generic bid that gives room for maneuvering. An example of the latter is this: "I am receiving a miraculous insight that is rejuvenating my life." You'll be focusing on your desire throughout the next steps.

STEP 2: **Conduct Spirit-to-Spirit.** Affirm your spirit, the helping spirits, and that of the greater Spirit. Keep your wish uppermost in your mind.

STEP 3: **Connect with a Source.** Request that the Spirit or your gatekeeper link you with a source that can inform you about your desire, as well as deliver the healing streams required to bring the aspiration into reality. Qualify the source as you've been shown how to do throughout this book.

STEP 4: **Gather Data.** Now ask the source whatever questions pop into your mind. What do you need to understand to actualize your desire? What energies must you be open to receiving? Is there an action you must perform to assure your manifestation? Keep asking questions, hearing the resulting insights either internally or externally, until you comprehend what is required to realize your dream.

STEP 5: **Open to the Streams.** Now ask that your source, along with the Spirit, generates and delivers streams of grace that will shift your energetics, as well as your body, mind, and soul, so you will attract the energies required to manifest your desire. Let the source provide you any additional illuminations, and bask in the infusion of energy as long as you want to.

STEP 6: **Close.** When you feel replete, thank all the helpers and allow the streams to separate you from the source. Return to your routine reality when ready.

Additional Tip

BOOST YOUR MANIFESTING BY RENEWING YOUR RED ZONE

In the first book in this series, *Subtle Energy Techniques*, I outlined four zones or stages experienced by a soul in relation to a single lifetime. One of these zones is called the red zone. Replenishing this energy body will imbue your system with the power needed to boost your manifesting process.

The red zone is an energy body that surrounds your physical body. It is equivalent to chakra 12 (depicted on figure 2) but can provide energy to any chakra, especially the first chakra. It looks like a liner that can increase or decrease in thickness. When you were conceived, the Spirit filled it with reams of life energy, the rocket fuel of life. The idea is that when you need extra oomph to get things done, the red zone energy will charge your first chakra, as if filling a gas tank or jumping a battery. In turn, the strengthened first chakra will activate your other chakras and fields. Your energetic boundaries will now be strong and resist drawing negative situations into your life. And if you program these fields with a manifesting message, you'll be more apt to get it noticed by and actualized within the world.

Unfortunately, the red zone "gasoline" can be depleted by stressful events and even stolen by others. This zone can also get jammed up with others' energies, which aren't good for us, or our own repressed emotions and memories. Most of us emerge from childhood with insufficient red zone energy and therefore limited manifesting abilities.

There are several ways to clean out and renew this zone. You can walk in nature, perform deep breathing, or use the quick and easy process in this tip. The following two-step process actually qualifies as a stand-alone healing and manifesting process, as it involves letting go of unnecessary energies (healing) and attracting beneficial energies (manifesting).

If you're ready to cleanse and activate your red zone toward a higher purpose, focus on a desire and conduct Spirit-to-Spirit. Ask the Spirit to send healing streams through your red zone, washing out your own and others' unnecessary or harmful energies. Then ask the Spirit to fill your red zone with overflowing amounts of life energy. The Spirit might even request that various natural beings perform this step for you, so don't be surprised if you sense the presence of beings related to plants, trees, flowers, elements, the stars, or the like.

The Spirit will now transport life energy from your red zone into your first chakra. Healing streams will distribute this life energy anywhere and everywhere it needs to go. Concentrate again on your desire and ask that the Spirit activate your desire with this red zone energy. The energy of your wish will emanate through your energy field and into the world so that all helpful and appropriate sources can respond to it. When you feel excited about the events that are assuredly about to occur, take a few deep breaths and return to your life.

CHAPTER 8

Additional Tip

CREATING A MIRACLE STONE

Remember our list of clairaudient-responsive stones from chapter 2? By infusing a stone with your verbalized manifesting desire, and by carrying this stone around with you, you can continually open your energetic system to beneficial energies. And if you want to supercharge the effect, instill the stone with the sound of the seed syllable that best relates to the wish.

First conduct exercise 18, Manifesting Through Clairaudience, and then follow it with these simple steps:

SELECT A STONE: Choose a stone listed in the
"Stones for Clairaudience" section on page 91
or select your own. This stone will serve as a
touchstone for the desire you focused on when
performing the manifesting exercise.

SOUND A DESIRE: Tonify the stone by stating, singing, or chanting your desire aloud while holding the stone in front of your mouth or heart.
Repeat your vocalization until you feel like the
stone is buzzing. The Spirit will cement this
energy in the stone with healing streams.

HUM A SEED SYLLABLE: To further potentize the
stone, return to the "Tones for Attunement"

section on page 93. Select the chakra that best matches the energy of your aspiration; you will be using the related seed syllable. For instance, if you are longing for a physical object, select the seed syllable for chakra one. Want romance? The fourth chakra bija is perfect. Now chant the chosen seed syllable directly into the stone, requesting that streams of grace seal your desire even more fully into the stone, which will now generate streams of grace continually until your dream is achieved.

CLOSE: Thank all involved for the blessings bestowed, and bring your enchanted stone wherever you go. This stone will keep the manifesting process alive in your subtle and physical bodies and your mind.

When your dream is achieved, you can place the stone in the sun, rain, or moonlight for a few hours and ask that streams of grace work through nature to cleanse it.

Additional Tip

WRITING DOWN THE BONES OF MANIFESTING

Guided and automatic writing are useful tools for staying on track while you're waiting for a manifestation to appear.

The truth is that manifesting usually requires involvement on our part. You can employ clairaudient writing to figure out what you're supposed to do to enable a manifestation and to evaluate for further action as time goes on.

After conducting exercise 18, Manifesting Through Clairaudience, set aside an hour a few days later. Check into your manifestation process. Have you already received what you desire? Then you can rejoice and continue on with your day, using that extra hour for fun. If you are still in process, it's time to create a manifesting plan using channeled writing.

Grab a writing instrument, conduct Spirit-to-Spirit, and ask the Spirit or your gatekeeper to align you with a manifesting advisor. Qualify this source; when you feel safe, ask it to remain with you until your desire is actualized. This source might also bring a task force of additional sources with it, providing you with depth and breadth of assistance.

After linking with your advisory head, invite the source to respond to these questions, which serve as qualifiers:

- Who or what are you?
- What divine specialty do you bring to my manifesting process?
- How are you going to help me?

- Are there other beings that will
  be working with me?

- Is there anything that you require from me?

Now work with this being to create a strategic manifesting plan, using questions such as the following as a framework and writing down the responses:

- What is the ultimate purpose of my
  manifesting desire?

- How will meeting it shift my life?

- What are the five to ten main action steps
  I'll need to take to actualize the desire?

- By which dates do I need to take each step?

- Are there attitudes or beliefs I need to hold or
  accept as truth in order to achieve these steps?

- How often should I check in with you, my
  advisor, to fine-tune my action steps?

- Are there any other questions I *should* be
  asking you in order to accomplish my goals?

Commit to checking in with your advisor through guided or automatic writing at the established times. Then, closing your eyes, ask for healing streams to adjust your energy. Return to your life when ready.

Questions for Assessing a Clairaudient Communication

What questions can be crafted from this chapter to assist you in your clairaudient communiqués? Following are ideas you can add to your ever-growing list, which will be summarized in the appendix.

- Should my clairaudience be used for a healing purpose?

- Should I apply my clairaudience to manifest a desire?

- Should I use my clairaudience to first perform a healing (or release energy) and then a manifestation (or attraction of energy)?

· · · · · · ·

Summary

Healing and manifesting are two of the most powerful applications of clairaudience. Healing involves the release of negative or unhelpful energies. Manifesting occurs when we attract useful or helpful energies. We can use these two processes together, as change usually requires letting go of what doesn't serve us in order to bring in something new.

· · · ·

CONCLUSION

A tree has fallen in the woods. There is a sound. Whether the tree drops right outside of your kitchen window or a thousand miles away, you can tune in to the event through your clairaudient ability.

You hear the tumbling of the tree, the chipping of the bark, and the rustling of the leaves on the ground moss. The chirping of disturbed birds, the slight rush of wind, and the chatter of the chipmunks: all these you perceive.

But there are other sounds. There is the swoosh of the tree's soul as it flies to the heavens and the soothing murmurs of the fairies in the glen. Maybe you even make out the singing of the Spirit, the Great Conductor who transforms every noise into a vital note in a beautiful composition.

A sound is just a sound unless it's so much more—that is, unless your clairaudience, the ability to perceive and create verbal psychic messages, is turned on and active.

Because of your clairaudience, you can harken to messages from the past, concurrent present realities, and the future. You can connect with the living and the deceased, as well as with beings or sources of information that are hard to categorize. You can overhear a personally insight-ful conversation in a restaurant and gain advice from an angel in a dream. You can do more than hear. You can listen. You can understand.

In these pages we focused on one of the three major mystical gifts: clairaudience. The other two abilities, which are clairempathy and clairvoyance, also crept into the work, as we can't totally separate one faculty from its brethren. One of the reasons is that all three mystical proficiencies employ our physical and subtle bodies, both of which process different versions of energy.

Energy is information that moves. Physical energy, which is measurable, is regulated by our physical body. Subtle energy, also called psychic, intuitive, or spiritual energy, is less measurable. It is managed by our subtle body.

In this book you learned how clairaudience relies on an integration between your physical and subtle bodies. Regarding the latter, it particularly employs your chakras, subtle organs that convert physical to subtle energy and vice versa, as well as the chakras' main partners, the auric fields. Every chakra houses its own psychic gift and depends on its correlated auric field to attract and dissem-inate subtle messages.

All clairaudient processes employ the fifth chakra and its related auric field. Located in the throat, the fifth chakra is our verbal center. Certain clairaudient techniques also utilize other pertinent chakras and fields as well. That's because subtle messages can be shared from center to center. A feeling can be translated as a poem and an image can help explain a song.

In this book you employed six clairaudient styles: classical clairaudience, speaking in tongues, clairaudient writing, telepathy, connecting with natural beings, and applying clairaudience for healing and manifesting purposes. This broad range of instruction has shown you that at any point you can obtain the verbal guidance needed to make decisions, improve your health, embrace love, and take purposeful action.

Sources of verbal information that support, educate, advise, warn, and uplift are always available. These sources are so varied that they are nearly impossible to catalogue. And isn't that wonderful? As displayed in this book, you can connect as easily with a being from the stars as the soul within your body. Clairaudience always centers on one overarching relationship: the one with Spirit. It is the bond between your own spirit and the Greater Spirit that enables you to steer your consciousness toward celestial realms and back, showing you how to hear but also listen and how to listen but also comprehend.

* * * *

APPENDIX A

Questions to Ask

At the end of each chapter, I shared questions reflecting the teachings in that chapter to aid you in every step of a clairaudient interaction. I have reshaped these questions so they can serve as a flow-through guide for an entire clairaudient activity, from calling upon a source to enabling it to perform healing or manifesting. Knowing that you might enter a clairaudient interaction at any place along the way, I've categorized the questions so you can jump in at any point.

Preparation

- Would it be appropriate for me to relate to a situation with my clairaudient skill?

- Is it time to perform Spirit-to-Spirit? (If yes, do so.)

- Should I also call upon healing streams of grace? (You can return to this question and ask for these streams at any time.)

- Should I be using my gatekeeper?
- Which of the following types of clairaudience would best serve my purpose:
  - ★ classical
    - — *receptive*
    - — *partial*
    - — *full*
  - ★ speaking in tongues
    - — *divine speaking*
    - — *language speaking*
  - ★ clairaudient writing
    - — *guided writing*
    - — *automatic writing*
  - ★ clairaudient telepathy
    - — *primal*
    - — *feeling-based*
    - — *mental*
    - — *spiritual (either spiritual empathy alone or with clairvoyance as well)*
  - ★ connection to natural beings
    - — *earthly (everyday, fantastical)*
    - — *otherworldly*

- ⋆ performance of healing
- ⋆ performance of manifesting
- ⋆ performance of healing and then manifesting
- Would a stone assist my clairaudient process?
- Would seed syllables assist my clairaudient process?

Qualifying a Clairaudient Sound

- Is this sound internal, external, or both?
- Is the sound primarily composed of any of the following:
  - ⋆ a voice or voices
    - – *my own*
    - – *another's*
  - ⋆ noise
  - ⋆ environmental sounds
  - ⋆ music
  - ⋆ chanting
  - ⋆ tones
  - ⋆ other: ringing, buzzing, humming, slamming, animalistic, etc.

- What type of message is this:
  - ⋆ historical?
  - ⋆ illuminating?
  - ⋆ advising?
  - ⋆ educational?
  - ⋆ futuristic?
- Am I sure this message is clairaudient or...
  (If it's not clairaudient, what should I do?)
  - ⋆ repetition of abuse?
  - ⋆ fantasy?
  - ⋆ others' energies?
  - ⋆ a mental challenge?

Qualifying the Source

- Is this source...
  - ⋆ worldly?
    - — *alive person or people*
    - — *deceased person or people*
    - — *"other" being (a soul waiting to be born)*
    - — *a natural being or beings*
    - — *the self*
    - — *part of the self*
    - — *part of another's self*
    - — *fantastical*

- ⋆ otherworldly?
  - — *divine (like an angel or demon)*
  - — *natural (like from another planet or dimension)*
- ⋆ Spirit–approved?
- ⋆ not Spirit–approved? (If not, what should I do?)
- What is the name of the source?
- What do these sounding factors tell me about the source?
  - ⋆ internal or external sound/voice
  - ⋆ own or other voice
  - ⋆ single or multiple sources
  - ⋆ past/present/future in origin
- What do these qualities of the sound or voice tell me about the source and its message?
  - ⋆ subjective/objective
  - ⋆ close/far
  - ⋆ pitch/timing/timbre/tone
- What do my feelings and bodily sensations tell me about the source or its message?
- What is the source's overarching message?
- Where do I go from here?

Clean Interactions

- Am I being affected by any of the following: (If so, shall I ask for healing streams?)
  - ★ energetic attachment?
    - — *cord*
    - — *curse*
  - ★ energetic wound?
- Am I experiencing any clairaudient red flags? (If so, what should I do?)
  - ★ short-term
  - ★ long-term
- What brain state am I in?
- Should I switch to a different brain state?

Gratitude

- How can I best remain open to grace-filled clairaudient insights?
- How can I best express my gratitude for the message provided?

APPENDIX B

Essential Energy Work Techniques

Here are the quick and easy steps needed to perform the signature techniques.

Spirit-to-Spirit

This easy three-step process centers you in your essential self, allows you to interact with the highest aspect of others, and turns your will over to a greater power. By using this technique, you invite only the best outcomes for self and others.

1. Affirm your personal spirit.

2. Affirms others' spirits, those seen and unseen.

3. Affirm the Spirit, which works toward the highest outcome for all concerned.

Healing Streams of Grace

Healing streams of grace pour endlessly from the Spirit. Once energetically connected to you or another, these streams will bring about the highest possible outcome. This promise relates to healing, manifesting, or obtaining guidance. Following are simple steps for requesting the universal streams for yourself or another.

1. Conduct Spirit-to-Spirit.

2. Ask the Spirit to send the correct healing streams of grace to self or other. These can also be beamed into an object, substance, or anything else.

3. Thank the Spirit for updating or changing these streams on an as-needed basis.

References

Advanced Tissue. n.d. "Frogs and Wound Healing."
https://www.advancedtissue.com/frogs-and-wound
-healing-whats-the-connection/

Al-Islam.org. n.d. "The Birth of Islam and the Proclamation
by Muhammad of His Mission."
https://www.al-islam.org/restatement-history-islam
-and-muslims-sayyid-ali-ashgar-razwy/birth-islam-and
-proclamation-muhammad

ASA Staff. n.d. American Society of Aging. "Bird Tales
Harnesses the Healing Power of Our Feathered Friends."
http://www.asaging.org/blog/bird-tales-harnesses
-healing-power-our-feathered-friends

Bynum, Edward. 2012. *Dark Light Consciousness*. Santa Fe:
Bear & Company.

Callaway, Ewen. 2009. "Foreign Accent Syndrome Doesn't
Mean Brain Damage." *Daily News*, June 3, 2009.
https://www.newscientist.com/article/dn17246-foreign
-accent-syndrome-doesnt-mean-brain-damage/

Dale, Cyndi. 2018. *Awaken Clairvoyant Energy.* Woodbury, MN: Llewellyn.

———. 2014. *The Spiritual Power of Empathy.* Woodbury, MN: Llewellyn.

———. 2017. *Subtle Energy Techniques.* Woodbury, MN: Llewellyn.

Dejean, Valerie. n.d. Spectrum Center. http://valeriedejean.org/tommy7.html

Dockrill, Peter. 2016. "Scientists Discover That Our Brain Waves Can Be Sent by Electrical Fields." *Science Alert,* January 15, 2016. http://www.sciencealert.com/scientists–discover–new –method–of–brain–wave–transmission–electrical–fields

Ellis, Marie. 2013. "How We Can 'Hear' Our Inner Voice." *Medical News Today,* July 2013. www.medicalnewstoday.com/articles/263428.php

Goodnet. n.d. "Five Animals with Incredible Healing Powers." http://www.goodnet.org/articles/5–animals–incredible –healing–powers–list

gotquestions.org. n.d. "What Is Glossolalia?" https://www.gotquestions.org/glossolalia.html

Hearing Voices Network. n.d. "Creative People Including Writers, Artists, and Musicians." https://hearingvoicescymru.org/positive–voices/famous –voice-hearers/creative-people/

Hearing Voices Network. 2018. "Famous People Who Hear Voices."
https://www.hearing-voices.org/voices-visions/famous-people/

HeartMath Institute. 2016. "Interconnectivity Tree Research Project." June 29, 2016.
https://www.heartmath.org/calendar-of-events/interconnectivity-tree-research-project/

IFL Science. n.d. "Brain-to-Brain Interfaces: The Science of Telepathy."
http://www.iflscience.com/brain/brain-brain-interfaces-science-telepathy/

Joseph, Rhawn, 1996. "The Mind & God of Adolf Hitler."
http://brainmind.com/Hitler.html

Kshatri, Jay. 2015. "Sound Healing…More Than Good Vibration." *Think Smarter World*, July 5, 2015.
http://www.thinksmarterworld.com/sound-healing-more-than-just-a-good-vibration/

————. 2016. "The Unseen Subtle Energy That Fills 96% of Our Existence." *Think Smarter World*, July 14, 2016.
http://www.thinksmarterworld.com/unseen-subtle-energy-fills-96-existence/

Lyons, Leslie. 2003. "Why Do Cats Purr?" *Scientific American*, January 27, 2003.
https://www.scientificamerican.com/article/why-do-cats-purr/

• • • •

Mauro, Colleen. 2015a. *Spiritual Telepathy: Ancient Techniques to Access the Wisdom of Your Soul.* Wheaton, IL: Quest Books.

Mauro, Colleen. 2015b. "Three Types of Telepathy." *Reality Sandwich*, July 9, 2015.
http://realitysandwich.com/317591/three-types-of
-telepathy/

McCarthy-Jones, Simon. 2012. *Hearing Voices.* New York: Cambridge University Press.

Medicine Hunter. n.d. "About Plant Medicines."
http://www.medicinehunter.com/about-plant
-medicines

Moisse, Katie. 2010. "Detected and Decoded Outside the Head." *Scientific American*, March 2, 2010.
https://www.scientificamerican.com/article/brain
-controlled-movement/

Mowbray, Mike. 2018. "Clairaudience." Sixth Sense.
http://sixthsensereader.org/about-the-book/abcderium
-index/clairaudience/

Near-Death Experiences and the Afterlife. 2016. "Biography of Edgar Cayce."
http://www.near-death.com/paranormal/edgar-cayce
/biography.html

REFERENCES

Smith, Colin. 2015. "Scientists Explain in More Detail How We Hear Via Bones in the Skull." Imperial College of London, July 9, 2015.
http://www3.imperial.ac.uk/newsandeventspggrp /imperialcollege/newssummary/news_9-7-2014-14 -58-1

Swain, Mike. 2012. "Scientists Find Way to Hear the Thoughts Inside Our Heads." *Mirror*, January 31, 2012.
https://www.mirror.co.uk/news/technology-science /science/scientists-find-way-to-hear-the -thoughts-659978

Underground Health Reporter. 2016. "DNA Science and What Russian Researchers Have Suprisingly Discovered…"
http://undergroundhealthreporter.com/dna-science -and-reprograming-your-dna/

Upthegrove, R., et al. 2016. "Auditory Verbal Hallucinations in First-Episode Psychosis: A Phenomenological Investigation." University of Bristol, *British Journal of Psychiatry Open*: 2, 88–89.
http://bjpo.rcpsych.org/content/2/1/88

Walia, Arjun. 2015. "5 Classic Experiments Showing Extremely Significant Results for Human Telepathy." *Collective Evolution*, August 4, 2015.
http://www.collective-evolution.com/2015/08/04/5 -classic-experiments-showing-extremely-significant -results-for-human-telepathy/

Order at
LLEWELLYN
.COM

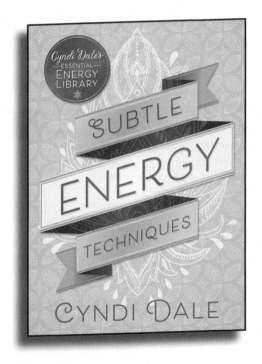

Subtle Energy Techniques
BOOK 1 OF CYNDI DALE'S
ESSENTIAL ENERGY LIBRARY

Cyndi Dale

Renowned author Cyndi Dale invites you into the world of subtle energy, where you'll explore auras, chakras, intuition, and the basics of her groundbreaking energy techniques. Whether your goals are physical, psychological, or spiritual, these methods can help you achieve your desires, heal your wounds, and live an enlightened life.

978-0-7387-5161-0
5 X 7 · 288 PP. · $14.99

Order at
LLEWELLYN
.COM

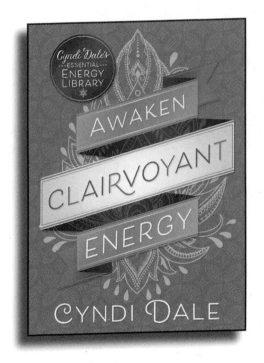

Awaken Clairvoyant Energy

Book 2 of Cyndi Dale's Essential Energy Library

Cyndi Dale

Attract more of what you love into your life, travel between lifetimes, connect with the deceased or a child yet to be born, and much more by using your clairvoyant talents. Renowned author Cyndi Dale reveals the secrets of clairvoyant energy and provides step-by-step instructions for six different clairvoyant styles. From healing and manifesting to clearing blocks, using future sight, and understanding the chakras, this wonderful guide helps you explore many topics and grow through the power of your energetic abilities.

978-0-7387-5162-7
5 X 7 · 288 PP. · $14.99

Order at
LLEWELLYN
.COM

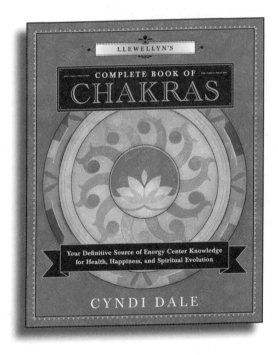

Llewellyn's Complete Book of Chakras

YOUR DEFINITIVE SOURCE OF ENERGY
CENTER KNOWLEDGE FOR HEALTH,
HAPPINESS, AND SPIRITUAL EVOLUTION

Cyndi Dale

As powerful centers of subtle energy, the chakras have fascinated humanity for thousands of years. *Llewellyn's Complete Book of Chakras* is a unique and empowering resource that provides comprehensive insights into these foundational sources of vitality and strength. Discover what chakras and chakra systems are, how to work with them for personal growth and healing, and the ways our understanding of chakras has transformed throughout time and across cultures.

Lively and accessible, this definitive reference explores the science, history, practices, and structures of our subtle energy. With an abundance of illustrations and a wealth of practical exercises, Cyndi Dale shows you how to use chakras for improving wellness, attracting what you need, obtaining guidance, and expanding your consciousness.

978-0-7387-3962-5
8 X 10 · 1,056 PP. · $39.99